Tomorrow's Transactions
The 2015 Reader

A selection of posts from the
Tomorrow's Transactions Blog from 2014

By David G.W. Birch

GW00566127

www.tomorrowstransactions.com/blog

Published in the United Kingdom in 2015 by:

Mastodon Press
Tweed House,
12 The Mount,
Guildford,
Surrey,
GU2 4HN.
England.
http://www.mastodonpress.com/

ISBN
Paperback: 978-0-9569236-7-7 Kindle 978-0-9569236-8-4

Printed in the UK by CPI William Clowes Ltd, Beccles, NR34 7TL.

You can contact Consult Hyperion at:
Consult Hyperion
Tweed House,
12 The Mount,
Guildford,
Surrey, GU2 4HN,
England.
Telephone: +44 (0) 1483 301 793
Fax: +44 (0) 1483 561 657
info@chyp.com
http://www.chyp.com

Contents

Preface

I hope you enjoy this collection of posts from the Tomorrow's Transactions blog for 2014 and look forward to your comments on the blog through 2015! In case you're wondering whether to read on or not, I think I can say that the blog proved to be a pretty useful resource for organisations looking at their transaction strategies last year. The Consult Hyperion "hot five" technologies for 2014 (that kick off Chapter 9) were, for the most part, pretty accurate. This ought to be no surprise, since as blook readers must realise, my colleagues here are always working on projects involving the exploitation of new technologies in the transactions business while I maintain the deceptive appearance of a blog based on random thoughts. As an example: my prediction that tokenisation would be hot in 2014 was a cheat, based on the fact that I knew just how much tokenisation work was already going on all around me down at CHYP End, not evidence for my crystal balls.

This year I've taken slightly different tack. I've chosen to highlight five areas where it is no secret that we are working on projects right now, but in a way I think even our clients may not have seen just how important the new technologies are and the extent to which their business strategies will be constrained by seemingly low-level technology discussions that will be made over the coming year. So, with that in mind, here are the "live five" for 2015 where I think clients should pay serious attention to technology decisions that are being made in the short term because of what they mean for business in the long term.

The first area is **in-app payments**. Much of the discussion around Apple Pay, tokenisation, NFC and retail has naturally focused on the "tap and pay" simplicity of the proposition. However, there are lots of reasons for thinking that this will be a sideshow rather than the main event. The introduction of tokenisation means that in-app payments ("app and pay") can now be more secure than chip and PIN payments and since I rather imagine that most retailers would prefer no POS to enhanced POS and given the experiences that we already see around us from Uber to AirBnB and KFC, I think that in-app payments will become the norm, the most frictionless way to pay. Once again, this is hardly a wild prediction since some major mobile commerce players (eg, Priceline) have already announced Apple Pay integration.

The second area is **re-localisation**. We've lived through a period where there has been great pressure for internationalisation and the globalisation of payment solutions. Nobody wants to travel with 100 different cards in their pocket and when I get off the plane in the US or Australia or anywhere else I expect to be able to use my Visa, MasterCard or American

Express card just as I do at home. However a combination of factors ranging from interchange regulation to in-app payments to non-bank players means that we will see a swing back toward more domestic solutions. In many parts of the world national payment solutions are seeing a resurgence, many of them looking at China Unionpay as an exemplar, but I think the trend toward multiple three-party systems instead of a small number of four-party systems means that we may see a return to payment systems that are owned and operated by retailers, brands and perhaps even local communities.

The third area is **privacy**. Once we have reasonable identification and authentication technology in place we can begin an intelligent discussion about how to use it. My observation is that for many of our clients the opportunity to make privacy part of their customer proposition, something that must be founded on strong security, is now a feasible business strategy. Privacy, as can already been seen in the actions of Apple and Google, is moving from a back-office hygiene factor to an integral component of consumer products.

The fourth is the **blockchain**. In parallel with a demand for privacy there is a growing demand for transparency. When you look at how a product like Venmo is evolving, you can see that certain groups within the population are opting for their own transparency and I think this represents an underlying and more general demand for transparency from institutions. Trading digital assets using an open distributed public ledger means a new way of trading that can combine privacy and transparency to create new and trusted markets.

The uniqueness of blockchain assets (the end of double-spending!) may mean that the impact of the technology is also felt in the physical. The fifth area of focus is ID for the Internet of Things, or **IDIoT** as I call it for short. I agree with the predictions I see all around me about the coming year being a turning point in the evolution of the Internet of Things and I see examples of new connectivity and new devices around me all the time. What I don't see is a security infrastructure emerging to manage those connections and manage those devices and this is where I think we may see intellectual effort rewarded in 2015. In fact, I can see that this might become the key focus area of the coming year as the Internet of Things comes together from digital assets that are traded transparently previously for the people involved in the trading, in-app transactions using a variety of local identity, and payment systems make for a seamless new environments of interaction and transaction.

About the author:

David G.W. Birch is a Director of Consult Hyperion, the IT management consultancy that specialises in electronic transactions. Here he provides specialist consultancy support to clients around the world, including all of the leading payment brands, major telecommunications providers, government bodies and international organisations including the OECD. Before helping to found Consult Hyperion in 1986, he spent several years working as a consultant in Europe, the Far East and North America. He graduated from the University of Southampton with a B.Sc (Hons.) in Physics.

He is is an internationally-recgonised thought leader in digital identity and digital money; was named one of *Wired* magazine's global top 15 favourite sources of business information, listed in the European *Power 50* for digital financial services, rated a NextBank *Fintech Titan* and ranked Europe's most influential commentator on the emerging payments field by *Total Payments*. His latest book "Identity is the New Money" was published in April 2014.

Acknowledgement:

This blook was only made possible by the hard work of my colleagues at Consult Hyperion. All I did was to listen to what they are talking about, see the incredible work they are doing for our clients and steal their ideas to turn into blog posts!

I've made some more changes to the organisation of those posts this year to reflect a change in the way that we organised the blog itself and given the great interest in Bitcoin and other cryptocurrencies this year I've pulled some relevant posts together in a separate subsection. The book is still in three sections (People, Money and Markets) as it was last year; a breakdown put in place to reflect our consulting work in the different market sectors, and I hope that this simple structure makes it easy to pick up and browse by groups of posts as well as by sections as a whole. Oh, and I hope you don't mind but I've taken out the reader comments: the blook was getting much too big and we needed to slim it down. The comments are, of course, still there on the blog for everyone to read!

Dave Birch, February 2015.

Part 1: People

Chapter 1: Identification and Authentication

It's really hard to work out what to do about digital identity. Should people be forced to use one digital identity, or should they be allowed many? Should that one be in their "real" identity or not? Instead of dealing with a complex topic properly, we seem to be switching between being paralyzed on one hand and panicked into making bad decisions on the other. One of the reasons for the complexity of the topic, I am sure, is that identity doesn't mean the same thing in the virtual world as in the mundane. Online identity is richer, more complex and more sophisticated than mundane identity. As I have constantly complained, both governments and businesses have yet to make the paradigm shift (I'm using the phrase in its genuine sense here, in the sense of a model of reality) and remain unable to resolve apparent paradoxes that vanish from a new, and better, perspective.

Biometrics are the answer, if you ask the right question (2ⁿᵈ April)

How did you pay for your last car? Or your last cup of coffee? Did you use different payment products or technologies for these different purposes? I didn't: I used my debit card for both. In order to buy the car, I just had to know the PIN. In order to buy the cup of coffee, I didn't have to know my PIN (or signature or anything else) but I did have to provide photo ID. As a consequence, it took longer to buy the coffee and was less convenient. Welcome to the world of payment authentication.

I don't think buying car using a chip and PIN card is remarkable or even interesting, by the way. I'm sure people do it all them time. Here's a chap in Canada who did it, for example.

> *Monaco, the founder and managing partner of a Toronto investment relations firm, alleges in his lawsuit that he discovered the charge of $81,276 "during a routine check of his Visa account balance" in June 2010.*

> *[From Bank customer's lawsuit raises questions about fraud liability - Canada - CBC News][1]*

---

[1] *http://www.cbc.ca/news/canada/bank-customer-s-lawsuit-raises-questions-about-fraud-liability-1.2561676*

So the guy bought a car with a chip and PIN card. As I said, we've done the same. When my wife bought her new car, we paid using chip and PIN. Having test driven the car, a used Peugot, and decided that she wanted it, we arranged to go and complete the sale. I called the dealer and asked if he wanted me send him the money over the interweb tubes (in the UK, we have the immediate settlement Faster Payment Service, FPS, so I could have sent him the money by PingIt or mobile banking with no trouble at all) and he said that no, a debit card would be fine. We drove down to dealership, signed the papers, I put by bank debit card into the terminal and entered by PIN[2]. Transaction accepted. I thought I might get a phone call from my bank just to double check that I was buying a $12,000 used car with my debit card, but I never did.

Compare and contrast this pleasant and quick purchasing experience with my most recent card purchasing experience in America where, as I mentioned before, I was required to produce photo ID to buy a $3 cup of coffee on my Simple card. As was Jim Bruene, who was similarly surprised by the state of payments in the US in 2014!

> *@dgwbirch wasn't making up coffee shop example. Just had to show photo id on $3.75 purchase. Waste of time/money. #payconnect*
>
> — *Jim Bruene (@netbanker) March 11, 2014*

It was more of a waste of time than you might imagine, since the photo ID I showed was an expired building pass for our New York office. Anyway, back to my point. If had a card with an $80,000+ credit limit and I used it to buy a car, even with a PIN, I would expect another authentication factor. Maybe an SMS to my phone, a message to my Amex app, something. I might even, for charges in excess of, let's say, $75,000, expect to have my picture taken or be required to use my iPhone fingerprint reader as an additional factor to confirm the transaction.

This is not because the iPhone fingerprint reader delivers James Bond-style nuclear-launch level identification. It doesn't, because it's about convenience. In fact it does not guarantee identification at all, but using Apple's TouchID as an additional and convenient authentication factor with the range of factors present in the mobile makes complete sense in risk management terms. And I think the public would be happy with it.

---

[2] *Actually, I know that I always say that I never buy anything with a debit card, but the dealership surcharged on credit cards. Since I figured I had ample warranty and associated legal protections, and that I was buying from a reputable dealership, and that the Avios or cashback that I would get weren't worth a fraction of the surcharge amount, I decided to use the debit card.*

The Tomorrow's Transactions Reader 2015

One in two people surveyed (49%) stated they would like to have biometric payments, such as fingerprint, palm or iris scanners, far outweighing the popularity of emerging mobile technology options.

[From Biometric payments are top option for security-concious shoppers, survey finds | Retail News][3]

What this means, other than customers have seen biometrics in Hollywood movies but not NFC, is unclear, but I do think that using biometrics as a convenience technology in authentication for retail payments makes complete sense.

"We expect to see biometrics becoming increasingly prevalent over the course of the next 3-4 years, driven by a desire among vendors and consumers alike to be better protected when accessing mobile services," summarised [Jean-Noel Georges].

[From Investorideas.com - Biometrics Can Revolutionise Mobile Payment Security, says Frost & Sullivan][4]

As our old chum Julian Ashbourn (you can listen to Julian in our podcast series points out in this excellent new book *Biometrics in the New World– The Cloud, Mobile Technology and Pervasive Identity*, there is a world of difference between using biometrics for identification and using them for authentication to establish entitlement. It is this latter mode, in combination with the mobile phone, that offers us a practical and cost-effective way forward.

We'll be giving Barclays the finger next year (5th September)

It was really fascinating to read today's reports about the "new" security technology that is going to be introduced by Barclays Bank in the UK for their corporate clients. Apart from anything else, Consult Hyperion is one of those corporate clients so we will undoubtedly be one of the users of this new-fangled login kit.

Just that you understand the context for the new technology: we are a "Small- or Medium-sized Enterprise" (SME) user of Barclays Banking and have been for a great many years. They provide us with smart card readers and we have two of these attached to PCs in our office. We also have four smart cards, each with its own PIN. Our two accounts staff have

---

[3] http://retailtimes.co.uk/biometric-payments-are-top-option-for-security-concious-shoppers-survey-finds/
[4] http://www.investorideas.com/news/2013/biotech/09041.asp

a card each as does our Finance Director and our HR director. To make an online payment, someone with a smart card has to instruct the payment and then somebody else with another smart card has to verify the payment. To be honest, the whole system works perfectly well and as far as I know we are happy with it. However, Barclays are adding convenience and higher security to their corporate banking service by moving to biometrics in the coming year.

> Barclays is introducing new finger scanning technology that will allow customers to access their online bank accounts and authorise payments without the need for PINs or passwords... The Barclays Biometric Reader will initially be available to Barclays Corporate Banking clients from 2015.

> [From Video: Barclays to introduce finger scans instead of PINs - Telegraph][5]

The technology that they are referring to here is the Hitachi finger vein scanning system. It works by having a user insert their finger into a device that uses a particular kind of light to scan the finger to obtain the pattern of veins under the skin. This pattern is stored inside a tamper resistant chip in the device and when the device is subsequently called upon to authenticate the user, their finger vein pattern is compared against the template. So starting next year, our staff will no longer need the smart card and the PIN, but will just put their finger in the scanning device.

The BBC were kind enough to invite me on to their lunchtime "You and Yours" magazine programme to discuss this innovation. I think they were a tiny bit surprised, to be honest, when I told them that the technology was eight years old! I also told them, in the spirit of openness and integrity that is associated with the good name of Consult Hyperion throughout the civilised world, that we had been retained by Hitachi some years ago to carry out a study on the security of this product and its suitability for certain financial services applications. I haven't actually been to the files to dig out the report, but I do remember that our guys were happy with the security and thought it appropriate in certain use cases. Here's what I wrote about the technology seven years ago:

> The vein authentication system has been available in the Japanese market since October 2006 and has already been deployed by Sumitomo Mitsui Banking Corporation as the user ID system for ATMs located in am/pm convenience stores throughout Japan

---

[5] http://www.telegraph.co.uk/finance/personalfinance/bank-accounts/11076131/Barclays-to-introduce-finger-scans-instead-of-PINs.html

The Tomorrow's Transactions Reader 2015

[From Fingering suspects - Tomorrow's Transactions][6]

As I understand it, there is an interesting heritage to the technology because in certain Asian countries people are uncomfortable with touching devices that are touched by lots of other people. This is why in some hotels in the Far East, I've noticed, as soon as you press the button in the elevator an attendant immediately gives a quick spray and wipes it off so that it is pristine for the next traveller. As a result, both Hitachi and Fujitsu looked to develop alternatives to the fingerprint scanners that were being developed in the West. Hitachi opted for finger vein and Fujitsu, if memory serves, opted for palm print. In both cases there is no contact between the finger or hand and the scanner which uses light to get its data.

As I told Peter White on the show, this is actually a very good use of biometrics. By and large, in the mass-market, we think that the use of biometrics as an authentication technology that uses a local template is broadly speaking a good idea and the use of biometrics as an identification technology against a remote template is broadly speaking a bad idea (because the templates can be stolen and reverse-engineered). In the case of the Fujitsu scanner, as in the case of the iPhone, the biometric template is stored locally in tamper-resistant hardware and is never given up. The template obtained by reading is fed into the tamper-resistant hardware for analysis and matching, which is a great way to do things.

I think what Barclays are doing here is an interim step that gives us a window into the more generalised solutions for the future where a variety of biometrics will be used for local authentication against devices and the devices will communicate the authentication through standard mechanisms (such as FIDO) into standard identity management systems. The fingerprint scanner on the iPhone and on the Samsung S5 seems to me a more likely mass-market choice than finger vein scanners but who knows.

Meanwhile, down at CHYP End, and we are looking forward to our new scanners arriving and you can rest assured that there will be pictures when they do!.

What does the Talmud tell us about ApplePay (23rd September)

As has become traditional at the Annual Consult Hyperion/NYPAY "Tomorrow's Transactions Unconference" hosted by the kind people at Google in New York, we started the day having an author give the kick-off talk followed by an onstage Q&A. This year it was the wonderful Jeffrey Robinson (known to you as the author of "The Laundrymen", a seminal work on money laundering) who read a little from his new book "BitCon".

---

[6] *http://tomorrowstransactions.com/2007/11/fingering-suspe/*

I had a vague suspicion that his view might be a tad controversial but since I learn fastest by hearing smart people argue I thought it worth the risk. It was.

In the afternoon we were honoured to be able to welcome Lisa Servon to the stage for a thought piece on the unbanked. Lisa wrote one of the best articles I've ever read on the topic (and I've read a lot because of Consult Hyperion's work in emerging markets and my work with the Bill & Melinda Gates Foundation's Financial Services for the Poor programme) and was kind enough to let me record one of the most interesting podcasts I ever recorded. Her thought-provoking views were exactly what was needed to get people at least noticing the box even if not thinking outside it.

I delivered the other of the afternoon thought pieces and chose to base it on the absolutely brilliant NPR Planet Money podcast (I strongly urge you to subscribe to their super series) on the topic of signatures for payment card transactions .

The signature. It's supposed to say, "This is me." But where did the idea come from? And why are we still using it? We consult a rabbi, a lawyer and a credit card executive.

[From Episode 564: The Signature : Planet Money : NPR][7]

Now the issue of signatures and the general use of them to authenticate customers for credit card transactions in the US has long been a source of amusement and anecdote. I am as guilty as everybody else is using the US retail purchasing experience to poke fun at the infrastructure there (with some justification, since as everybody knows the US is responsible for about a quarter of the world's card transactions but half of the world's card fraud) but I've also used it to illustrate some more general points about identity and authentication. Forum friend Brett King wrote a great piece about signatures a few months ago in which he also made this more general point about authentication mechanisms for the 21st-century.

In a recent UN/ICAO commissioned survey on the use of signatures in passports, a number of countries including the UK recommended phasing out the long held practice because it was no longer deemed of practical use.

[From Why Kids don't have signatures — Medium][8]

---

[7] *http://www.npr.org/blogs/money/2014/08/29/344034815/episode-564-the-signature*
[8] *https://medium.com/@brettking/why-kids-dont-have-signatures-93b9aaac1772*

The Tomorrow's Transactions Reader 2015

Now, as Ronald Mann (the Colombia law professor interviewed for the show) quite accurately points out, card signatures are really all about distributing liabilities for fraud transactions. He called them "eccentric relics", a phrase I loved and will use without limit. The system doesn't really care whether I sign my transaction Dave Birch or Segio Aquero: all it cares is that it can send the chargeback the right way (bank or merchant, essentially) when it comes. I think there are far better and more cost-effective ways of doing this, and we'll come back to them in a minute.

In addition to the usual comments about cardholder verification methods that you might expect to hear from a lawyer and a payment scheme representative, the team went to ask a Talmudic scholar about signatures.

(The Talmud is the written version of the Jewish oral law and the rabbinic commentary on it that was completed in its current form some time in the fifth century. There are two parts to it: the oral law itself, which is known as the Mishnah, and the record of the rabbis arguing about it and what it meant, which is known as the Gemara.)

The Talmud, it turns out, is admirably clear about the use of signatures. The purpose of the signature is to identify the person. The scholar made a very interesting point about this, when he was talking about the signatures that are attached to the Jewish marriage contract, the Ketubah, pointing out that it is the signatures of the witnesses that have the critical function in dispute resolution. The signatures are used to track down the witnesses so that they can attest as to the ceremony taking place and as to who the participants were.

The show narrator made a good point about this, which is that it might make more sense for the coffee shop to get the signature of the person behind you in the line than yours, since yours is essentially ceremonial whereas the one of the person behind you has that Talmudic forensic function. One possibility, then, for a crowdsourced future retail payment mechanism would be to simply get a random person in the store to take a photo of you buying stuff and putting in escrow for 180 days before deletion in case the charge is disputed!

This set me thinking.

When it comes to making a retail transaction, my signature is utterly unimportant. This is why transactions work perfectly well when I either do not give a signature (for contactless transactions up to £20 in the UK, for example, or for no-signature swipe transactions in the US) or give a completely pointless signature as I do for almost all US transactions, either just scribbling an irrelevant line or carefully printing Sergio Leonel "Kun" Aguero Del Castillo (when I can make it fit).

But now consider a more generalised version of this experience when the future retail transaction is a witnessed exchange of data between my computer (for the sake of argument, my mobile phone) and the store's computer (for sake of argument, their iPad). Not only is there no need for me to sign this transaction, there's no need for me to enter a PIN code either, since the phone already knows that I am its rightful owner because I've already used the passcode or a fingerprint or whatever to unlock it. And it would be pointless if the clerk gave their signature to the transaction since what my mobile phone wants is the digital signature that it can actually validate to know that it is talking to a real and accredited store and that the payment has been properly recorded and acknowledged. This may well be the genius of ApplePay: since there are no signatures or PINs or anything else at all, it will very hard to make a more convenient experience for consumers.

The Talmudic scholar also mentioned in passing that according to the commentaries on the text, the wise men from 20 centuries ago also decided that all transactions deserved the same protection. It doesn't matter whether it's a penny or £1000, the transaction should still be witnessed in such a way as to provide the appropriate levels of protection to the participants. The Talmud says that every purchase is a big purchase. So, goodbye to electronic cash and goodbye to chip and PIN and hello to biometric authentication and secure elements: we have the prospect of a common payment experience in store, on the web and in-app: you click "pay" and your phone asks you to confirm and you put your finger on the home button. For everything: the cup of coffee and the pair of shoes and the plane ticket. It turns out that once again we can go back to the future in the design of our next retail payments system.

Authentication expectations are changing rapidly (1st October)

I've become converted to TransferWise for sending money between my UK and US bank accounts. It's a great service and I like their app. But I had a bit of a shock when I last opened my TransferWise app and discovered a TouchID log in.

Great, I thought, and carried on without paying much attention. What had happened, of course, was that the iOS 8 version of the app used TouchID because Apple opened the API up for developers and now they can take advantage of it. The very next app I opened was my Telegraph Fantasy Football app, which asked me for a user name and password.

I was infuriated by this and so couldn't be bothered any more. And afterwards, I couldn't help but reflect on how quickly this had happened. A couple of days after installing iOS 8 and already I can't be bothered to use apps that make me enter a username and password. Interesting, I thought, but put the thought to one side. Then, later in the day, I went to check a personal e-mail account and discovered I didn't know my password at all.

I forgot that Google made me change my e-mail password and I couldn't remember what I'd changed it to. And then I thought: screw this, I can't be bothered. It's getting worse. I've been getting more and more annoyed all day. I tried to upload a photo to our corporate Flickr account, and did a password reset (since I didn't know what the password was) only to discover it was sent to the e-mail address of someone who hasn't worked for the company for about three years.

Here's what should have happened, of course. I go to the Flickr site and select "Apple ID" or whatever. Since Safari knows what my Apple ID is, Apple can send a message to my iPhone to pop up a screen telling me that Flickr wants to authenticate and asking me to use TouchID. My fingerprint is recognised and - hey presto - I am automagically logged in to Flickr.

There are two reasons why this is such a huge step forward (even though, in security terms, the fingerprint authentication is not the most secure of all possible mechanisms). The first is that it means old and forgetful people like me don't have to remember passwords any more. The second is that I don't need to use two hands to log in, which I normally do with a username and password (because I transfer the phone to my right hand and type with my left, or alternatively type slowly and frequently inaccurately with my left thumb). I was playing with a prototype that our HyperLab guys built for another project last week and it was similarly easy to use the built-in Trusted Execution Environment (TEE) FIDO client on the Samsung S5 with fingerprint authentication, thus delivering a standard authentication infrastructure that means real convenience. I think this is going to spread quickly.

I say that because I was completely unprepared for how quickly I have become frustrated with apps that use "conventional" authentication. It's only a matter of time before I simply will not bother with any that stay with it.

Flatwood, ironware and cheap tin trays (19th November)

We tend to think about identity fraud as something involving human beings, but as "The Internet of Things" (or "IoT") expands, identity fraud will increasingly affect stuff as much as people. In fact, it already does.

In July, almost 700 ships worldwide engaged in identity fraud, which has grown 30 percent in the past two years... To hide their crimes on the high-seas, these ships broadcast false identities by using transmitters taken from scrapped vessels on the black market and by typing in made-up ID numbers.

[From The Chinese Ship That Sailed Over Land and Other Ways Vessels Lie - Bloomberg][9]

Who knew! There is maritime so-called IoT fraud rampant even as I type. I had absolutely no idea that ships had identity devices on board, but I suppose the idea is to help the Somali pirates to work out which ships to attack and which ships to leave alone.

Fifteen percent of all ships transmitting fake identities are tankers, typically carrying oil or oil products.

[From The Chinese Ship That Sailed Over Land and Other Ways Vessels Lie - Bloomberg]

Fascinating. There are tanker-loads of looted and expropriated oil pottering along the sea-lanes of the world masquerading as quinquiremes of Nineveh, illegal fishing boats masquerading as stately Spanish galleons and hulls laden with sanctions-busting weaponry masquerading as dirty British coasters. You really do learn something every day.

This Automatic Identification System (AIS) was designed to promote safety and avoid collisions by giving ships information on nearby vessels that might not be visible due to distance, bad weather conditions, or in crowded seas.... over the past year, there has been a 30% rise in AIS manipulation of IMO numbers (a ship's identity number, which is not supposed to change throughout its 'lifetime'), with over 1% of the AIS-transmitting ships now reporting false identification data.

[From One in a hundred ships using fake AIS identities as manipulation increases | defenceWeb][10]

As far as I can tell, everywhere that the IoT pops up — from health to transport to home control to in-car — it pops up with no security infrastructure (and, by the way, a password isn't security).

The Internet of Things (IoT), despite being decades old in concept, is a muddle of emerging technologies with unnerving

---

[9] http://mobile.bloomberg.com/news/2014-10-28/the-chinese-ship-that-sailed-over-land-and-other-ways-vessels-lie.html
[10]

http://www.defenceweb.co.za/index.php?option=com_content&view=article&id=3
6672:one-in-a-hundred-ships-using-fake-ais-identities-as-manipulation-increases&catid=108:maritime-security&Itemid=233

social, legal and moral implications, set in motion as the Internet and wireless became pervasive and sensor chips affordable.

[From Wearable Technology: Better Looking But As Unnerving And Confusing As Rest of Internet Of Things][11]

There are no standards, no authentication, no audit, no identity infrastructure at all. The Internet of Everyone Else's Things IOEET is a Chernobyl, people, a Chernobyl. I said this recently when the good people at Imperial College invited me along to give a guest lecture in their Smart Cities series. It was originally going to be called "Privacy in the Digital City" but I came up with that much better title, the IOEET, my comment on the rush to build the IoT without having a realistic plan for securing and managing this new infrastructure. It's one thing to joke about smart fridges, and who can resist it, but it's not about fridges it's about everything. And, a point I made eight years ago, it's really not clear to me that IoT deployment is rational or, at the moment, useful.

In the UK, we're already looking at using RFID in hospitals, but for tracking important things like equipment, not patients.

[From Insurers Study Implanting RFID Chips in Patients][12]

In the mass market, IoT deployment will, of course, have to be something that co-opts consumers to police it. When it's something like wine labels, you can see why people will co-operate to make it work.

After all, who wants to be embarrassed serving a fake wine at dinner and, aside from that, who doesn't want to learn more about a wine that they try and like?

[From The internet of things needs some thinking through]

But how can they trust it? How do you know if the ID of your wine is real or fake? What if you don't want your guests to know which wine they are being served? Putting IDs into things, whether ships or bottles of wine or blood pressure monitors is not, by itself, the solution. We are missing a whole layer that needs to sit on top of the "things".

How do we turn tags on and off? How do we grant and revoke privileges? How do we allow or deny requests for product or provenance?

---

[11] *http://www.forbes.com/sites/sarahcohen/2014/07/29/wearable-technology-better-looking-but-as-unnerving-and-confusing-as-rest-of-internet-of-things/?partner=yahootix*
[12] *http://tomorrowstransactions.com/2006/08/insurers_study_/*

[From <u>The internet of things needs some thinking through</u>][13]

Now, as I have previously written, the way forward is to trust the provenance rather than the product. The ID of the wine bottle is only useful to me if I can go online and see whether that ID is real, where the bottle was bought from, where it was bottled and so on and so forth. When it comes to consumer products, in security terms this means only one thing.

The counterfeiters will inevitably shift their attention to attacking the database.

[From <u>Digital Identity: There's whiskey in the jar-o</u>]

Is Bitcoin the solution here too then? Perhaps we might all be getting a little carried away about potential uses of the blockchain to make trustless infrastructure for the greater good, but I have strong suspicion that there is going to be a relationship between blockchain technology and IoT technology, because we need a means to ensure that virtual representations of things in the mundane cannot be duplicated in the virtual. We can do this in three ways as far as I know: a database, tamper-resistant hardware or blockchain. It's for the market to determine which method will deliver the right balance of cost and functionality.

P.S. For those of a literary bent, the title and ship descriptions in this post come from the John Masefield poem "Cargoes", which I (and a great many other British schoolchildren of the era) had to learn by heart when small.

Sometimes money is the new identity (24th November)

A guest post from Consult Hyperion Associate Victoria Richardson.

I'm a big fan of City Car Club. I don't have a car because mostly, I don't need one as I'm a short walk to trains and buses. But City Car Club fits the bill for occasions where it's just easier to travel by car. As well as being super convenient for people like me living the suburban dream, it makes a great case study about how payment and identity services are evolving in the UK.

The sign up process is the trickiest part and somewhat insightful as to the challenges that businesses face if they want to remotely verify specific customer attributes. Before letting me loose on the roads in one of their cars, clearly City Car Club needs to know whether I have a valid driver's

---

[13] *http://tomorrowstransactions.com/2013/11/the-internet-of-things-needs-some-thinking-through/*

license and how many points I have on this license. They do this by setting up a three-way call with the Driver and Vehicle Licensing Agency (DVLA). City Car Club calls me, then they patch in DVLA and I agree to DVLA divulging information about my driver's license. This must be a hugely costly process for City Card Club and one that will surely be replaced by a digital process, just as soon as Gov.UK Verify gets going.

Once you get over the clunky sign up process (which is no fault of City Car Club's), it's plain sailing. Using the slick app, which is protected by a four digit passcode, you select the location of the car you want (there are three within a few minutes walk of my house), the date and start/finish time and that's it. As you've already linked a credit card to your account at sign up, there's no additional payment step. Your card is charged at the end of your journey once a final calculation has been made, based on the actual length of the booking (you can extend a booking from the app if you need extra time) and mileage.

Accessing the car is simple too. City Car Club sends you a contactless membership card through the post and this is how you unlock the car. There's a contactless reader fixed to the inside of the windscreen, which you tap with your card. Once inside the car, you open the glove compartment, tap your passcode into a nifty piece of hardware which releases the physical key to the car and also lets City Car Club remotely control the car. In City Car Club lingo it's the "onboard computer".

What makes City Car Club so interesting from a payment card perspective though is that (as I discovered last weekend in a moment of panic when I realised three minutes before my booking was due to start, that of course I had lost my membership card) anything with a standard contactless interface (i.e., ISO/IEC 14443) can be used to open the car (once it has been linked to your account of course). So now my RBS debit card is the key to my City Car Club but I could equally have used my Oyster Card.

The customer experience here is great. There's no replacement membership card fee (for me or City Car Club) and no delay waiting for a new card to come through the post. In order to set my debit card as the key to the car, I pressed "phone Clubhouse". I told City Card Club that I had lost my membership card and they logged this against my account. Then, when I got to the car, I simply tapped my contactless debit card on the windscreen and the card reader took the serial number of the chip, and associated the card with my account. Once inside the car I punched my passcode into the "onboard computer", confirming the link between me and the card.

It's hugely encouraging to see new services built on the existing payments infrastructure that deliver a better customer experience as well as cost savings to the service provider. Now I'm just waiting for it all to end up on my phone, with some magic from Apple Pay.volutpat.

My phone knows your phone (9ᵗʰ December)

You might think I'm biased, but as has become clear to me from some of the projects that my colleagues at Consult Hyperion have been working on recently -- for banks, schemes, acquirers etc -- identity is moving up the strategic priority list. It's becoming a strategic issue for a great many businesses and a great many parts of businesses. Steve Shoaff from UnboundID summarised this rather neatly when he said that

> *Every customer-facing business is in the identity business; whether they know it or not*

> *[From Privacy Identity Innovation PII 2014: Insights on the "Economics of Identity" | UnboundID Blog][14]*

The corollary to this is, of course, that control over identity is becoming an actual battleground and it is not at all clear, even to those of us who follow developments obsessively, who is going to win. I suppose we rather lazily used to assume that it would be governments (the "continental" model) or banks (the "Scandinavian" model) who would step in to provide the kind of identity that we need to function in the new, online economy. Since they haven't, it's been clear for a while that there is potential for others to step in. I use my British Passport now and then, but I might use my Waitrose Passport or my LinkedIn Passport or my Microsoft Passport (I know, I know) a great deal more frequently.

> *Who wants to be an Identity Provider? A lot more companies than know it today.*

> *[From Identity Assurance: Who wants to be an Identity Provider? - Identity, Privacy and Trust][15]*

This isn't just about companies becoming identity providers. They will also become identity consumers. If Oprah Winfrey walks into your handbag shop then you want to know about which of her many forms of identification and authentication are in play. It might be face recognition. It might an app on her phone. It might be the phone company. It might be her smart watch or Google Glass or Fitbit of whatever.

---

[14] *https://www.unboundid.com/blog/2014/11/20/privacy-identity-innovation-pii-2014-insights-on-the-economics-of-identity/*
[15] *http://www.computerweekly.com/blogs/the-data-trust-blog/2013/01/identity-assurance-who-wants-t.html*

The Tomorrow's Transactions Reader 2015

The Black Eyed Peas star posted a series of tweets hitting out at United Airlines after reportedly being told to leave a VIP lounge because staff thought he had a fake membership card.

[From Will.i.am. launches furious Twitter rant after he is 'kicked out of first class airport lounge' | Mail Online][16]

I didn't pay any attention to this is because a) it was in the Daily Mail, so I took it for linkbait rather than news, b) I'd never heard the Black Eyed Peas (so I went on YouTube - let me tell you, the Pink Fairies they are not) and c) I don't know who William is. When I mentioned this on Twitter, a correspondent wrote to tell me that he had recently been in a meeting with him and his name is actually Will.i.am -- I don't know why -- and had found him to be a) really smart and b) really nice. But I was putting together some notes for my keynote on recognition as a key trend in the retail space for the Customer Festival down in Melbourne last year, so the reason I made a mental note of it was because William clearly had a smartphone with him (he was tweeting) and I didn't understand why this wasn't used to solve the problem (the problem of demonstrating that the person at the counter had the attribute IS_IN_MILEAGEPLUS). Maybe he's not on LinkedIn.

When I go to the BA lounge at one airport or another — where, by the way, I saw Paul Calf the other day and he wasn't able to find a seat for lunch any more than I was — they scan the barcode presented by my BA app. Surely United staff could have an app that could check William's app. I doubt it will be that long before the BA lounge will sprout Bluetooth beacons so that my app opens automatically as I walk into the lounge and does the necessary mutual authentication to enable me to get to the scones and jam unhindered.

The development of the smart phone as a tool for document verification and authentication has major implication for the industry

[From Authentication and the Smart Phone Revolution — Counting On Currency][17]

I agree completely, especially when the documents being authenticated are actually other smartphones.

---

[16] http://www.dailymail.co.uk/tvshowbiz/article-2625225/Will-launches-furious-Twitter-rant-kicked-class-airport-lounge.html
[17] http://countingoncurrency.com/wp/2012/10/22/authentication-and-the-smart-phone-revolution

Chapter 2: Social Media and Society

Social media has, in a very short time, become integral to society, It is now impossible to imagine any form of organisation that has not been fundamentally changed because of it. Everything from national politics to local hobby groups hangs off of the Internet but through the layer of social media. As a consequence, the nature of the transactions facilitated through social media is of great interest to those of us trying to build future-relevant, secure transactional systems right now..

Politicians just don't understand the Internet (14th January)

At the end of last year the nice people at Information Risk Management invited me along to their "Risky Business" event[18] in London to enjoy a morning of serious thinking about some key issues in information security. They had some pretty impressive speakers: Mike Lynch, the founder of Autonomy; the head of cyber policy for GCHQ, the head of IT security from the London Olympics and so on. The reason I was thinking about this was because I was thinking about the issue of Internet "filtering", as is now the fashion in the UK.

> *If their parents have chosen this option, children using O2 phones will be unable to access almost all of the internet: police websites, the NHS, ChildLine, the NSPCC, the Samaritans, many schools and even the main government website, GOV.UK.*

> *[From Some websites should be unblockable - Adrian Short][19]*

These problems are inevitable. But what do we want? Do we want children to be able to see things like MTV online? Who gets to decide? What is the principle at work? Alec Ross, who was Senior Advisor for Innovation and Technology to the Secretary of State Hilary Clinton, gave the keynote address on "The promise and peril of our networked world". I was looking forward to this, as I think that it's important to understand what the State Department's policies around security, privacy, the web and filtering are. Alec was a good speaker, as you'd expect from someone with a background in diplomacy, and he gave some entertaining and illustrative examples of using security to help defeat Mexican drug cartels and Syrian assassins. He also spent part of the talk warning against an over-reaction to "Snowden" leading to a web Balakanisation that helps no-one.

---

[18] *http://www.irmplc.com/event/risky-business-conference/*
[19] *http://adrianshort.org/2013/12/22/some-websites-should-be-unblockable/*

I was thinking about policy though. Governments, and people, don't really know what they want us (ie, technologists) to do. This is what I have casually referred to as the "Clinton Paradox" before, and it is nicely summarised here:

> *We must have ways to protect anonymity of good people, but not allow anonymity of bad people.*
>
> *[From Digital Identity: May 2011]*[20]

I challenged Alec about this in the Q&A — slightly mischievously, to be honest, because I suspected he may have had a hand in the speech that I referred to in that blog post — and he said that people should be free to access the internet but not free to break the law, which is a politician's non-answer (if "the law" could be written out in predicate calculus, he might have had a point, but until then...). If we take that at face value, though, what does it mean? Alec wasn't clear if he means just US law or anyone's law. We didn't get to discuss that.

When I pushed on the issue of openness, he was clearer. He said that he thought that citizens should be able to communicate in private even if that means that they can send each other unauthorised copies of "Game of Thrones" as well as battle plans for Syrian insurgents. I think I probably agree, but the key here is the use of the phrase "in private". I wonder if he meant "anonymously"? I'm a technologist, so "anonymous" and "private" mean entirely different things and each can be implemented in a variety of ways.

The politicians are going to have to tell us what they want. If they want people to be able to communicate anonymously, then they are going to have to accept that criminals will do so. If they want us to be able to communicate in private, then they are going to have to introduce an identity infrastructure and tell us under what circumstances the state will be able to "undo" that privacy.

It was an enjoyable and thought-provoking morning, so thanks for that IRM, but it left me slightly pessimistic that the gap between people like me and the people who are running things is widening. Is this an age thing?

GDP will grow in an electronic economy (5th March)

A fascinating roundtable at my favourite financial services think-tank, the Centre for the Study of Financial Innovation (CSFI), which had been

---

[20] *http://digitaldebateblogs.typepad.com/digital_identity/2011/05/*

selected by Diane Coyle for the launch of her new book "GDP: A Brief but Affectionate History: A Brief Affectionate History". The essence of the discussion was that GDP may still be useful in some circumstances, but it is too often used for purposes that it was never designed for and is manifestly not suited to. It wasn't until I was reading Diane's book on the train home that I realised just how arbitrary the concept and definition of GDP is, something reinforced in this week's excellent Planet Money podcast on "The Invention of the Economy" (which also includes comment from Diane).

With Diane was Joe Grice, who is Director and Chief Economist at the Office of National Statistics (ONS). I got to ask Joe whether it was true that government statistics on the UK economy do not measure computer games design (at which the UK does rather well) while keeping accurate count of whale oil production as alleged by NESTA...

> But existing data is pretty bad when it comes to new, fast-moving businesses. There's a SIC code for whale oil production, but good luck finding one for video games development or graphene.

> [From Big Data for better innovation policy | Nesta][21]

If you're wondering what an SIC code is, it's the Standard Industrial Classification code used to collect statistics for the ONS. Joe didn't get to answer because I asked a supplementary question about sustainability, relating to another of Diane's key points about innovation, and we went down another route.

Some of the questions were about measurement, and some of these were about money. One of the questions was about money and measurement. Someone asked, essentially, why the government doesn't just measure all of the money flows in the economy and use that actual data instead of yonks old statistical estimates that often need revised (most famously, as Diane noted, when Dennis Healey went cap in the hand to the IMF because Britain was in recession, only to discover when the figures were later updated that it wasn't). This reminded me of the old Robert Heinlein science fiction novel "Beyond This Horizon", in which cash is extinct and all payments run through computers and all the computers are connected to the government computer so the government can twiddle the nobs and dials to keep the economy on course. One might imagine certain other benefits of this electronic economy as well.

> "The current collection model brings with it a VAT Gap due to e.g. VAT fraud, insolvencies, mistakes by the taxable persons in the VAT return and VAT avoidance schemes. Desk research

---

[21] http://www.nesta.org.uk/blog/big-data-better-innovation-policy

*shows that the VAT Gap for 2009 can be cautiously estimated at
6,9% of GDP and 12% of total VAT liability in the EU-27. This
means that, in the EU-27, a total of EUR 118,8 billion has
according to those estimates not been collected by the tax
authorities in 2009."*

[From <u>118,8bn euros lost in 2009</u>][22]

No wonder the taxes I pay as a middle-England wage-slave are so high
when half the population are on the fiddle. Not only would electronic
money cut my tax bill, it would stop the ridiculous cross-subsidy from the
lawful to the lawless that plagues our moral fibre. But my point is that if
the black economy were turned white, UK GDP would grow by 20% or
so. And if you think I'm joking, let me observe that Joe said that there is
work underway to look at estimating the illegal drugs trade and
prostitution as components of GDP in compliance with EU rules.

*The Office for National Statistics is expected to comply with new
EU rules by revealing its first estimates for the size of the illegal
industries and how it has reached these calculations as soon as
March or April. Prostitution in Britain is set to be valued at
around £3 billion a year while the drug dealing sector is set to be
valued at £7 billion...*

*[From <u>Prostitutes And Drug Dealers 'Add £10 Billion To UK
National Wealth'</u>]*[23]

How much better it would be for the Chancellor of the Exchequer to have
accurate figures in his dashboard each morning rather than estimates? As a
complete aside, by the way, Heinlein was a bit of a visionary in more ways
than one. In 1939, he wrote that:

*There has grown up in the minds of certain groups in this country
the notion that because a man or corporation has made a profit
out of the public for a number of years, the government and the
courts are charged with the duty of guaranteeing such profit in
the future, even in the face of changing circumstances and
contrary to public interest. This strange doctrine is not supported
by statute or common law. Neither individuals nor corporations
have any right to come into court and ask that the clock of history
be stopped, or turned back.*

[From <u>Copyright wars are damaging the health of the internet</u>][24]

---

[22] *http://www.finextra.com/community/fullblog.aspx?id=4774*
[23] *http://www.huffingtonpost.co.uk/2014/02/10/prostitution-drugs-uk-
gdp_n_4758825.html*

The Tomorrow's Transactions Reader 2015

What Heinlein means is this. You used to make money out of farming, you don't any more: tough. You used to make money out of recorded music, you don't any more: tough. You used to make money out of transaction fees, you don't any more: tough.

Facebook money is overdue (16th April)

A couple of years ago my son was, as is rather the fashion with teenagers, in a band. With some friends of his, he arranged a "gig" (as I believe they are called) and a local venue. There were five bands involved and the paying public arrived in droves, ensuring that a good time was had by all. All of this was arranged through Facebook. All of the organisation and all of the coordination was efficient and effective so that the youngsters were able to self-organise in an impressive way. Everything worked perfectly. Except the payments.

When it came to reckoning up the gig wonga, we had a couple of weeks worth of "can you send PayPal to Simon's dad" and "he gave me a cheque what do I do with it?" and "Andy paid me in cash but I need to send it to Steve" and so on. Some of them had bank accounts, some of them didn't. Some of them had bank accounts that you could use online and others didn't. Some of them had mobile payments of one form or another and others didn't. I can remember that at one point my son turned to me and asked *why can't I just send them the money on Facebook?*

I didn't have a good answer to this, since I thought sending the money through Facebook would be an extremely good idea and I can remember discussing with some clients at the time what sort of services they might be able to offer to Facebook or other social networks that were empowered through an Electronic Money Issuing (ELMI) license and Payments Institution (PI) licence. As a fairly typical parent I would be much happier to use my credit card to load £20 onto a Facebook account that I could send to the kids for them to use online rather than give them my credit card details or allow them to use their own debit card details online. Hence I wasn't at all surprised to read that:

> Facebook is reportedly "only weeks away" from receiving regulatory approval as an e-money provider in Ireland, authorisation that would be valid throughout the European Union. Users in European countries could use Facebook accounts on their smartphones to send money home to friends and family in emerging markets.

---

[24] *http://m.guardian.co.uk/technology/blog/2013/mar/28/copyright-wars-internet*

[From Facebook plans mobile money serviceMobile World Live][25]

I remember writing a couple of years ago that I thought Facebook money could easily become the biggest virtual currency in the world given that there are so many people with Facebook accounts and the ability to send value from one account to another via Facebook would be attractive. Facebook did indeed launch "Facebook Credits" but they weren't really a currency, just a way of pre-paying for virtual goods with the service. A virtual currency is something more, true electronic money that you can send from one person to another.

Hence the ELMI. Now, as the FT pointed out, this is not actually a big deal for an organisation such as Facebook since any reasonably well-funded organisation can easily comply with the requirements but it's nevertheless a step for them to go out and get one and I hope it means that some fun and exciting new products are around the corner.

> *Obtaining an e-money authorisation in Ireland would require Facebook to hold capital of €350,000 and segregate funds equivalent to the amount of money it has issued, according to legal experts.*

[From Facebook targets financial services - FT.com][26]

Incidentally, the FT article also mentions that Facebook were looking at working with Azimo. I'm not surprised - and I'll tell you why. I had excellent fun last year at the 2nd annual PayExpo Dragon's Den. Our good friends at Clarion were kind enough to ask me to chair again and along with my fellow judges Mark Beresford from Edgar Dunn, David Parker from Polymath and Robert Courtneidge from Locke Lord I heard three finalist pitches:

Azimo, which I thought was a nicely done remittance play.

Pktmny, which as I recall was a new incarnation of the Visa Buxx / family accounts kind of proposition, and was rather nicely executed.

Itemize, a receipting white label. They were good sports when I described them as an NSA PRISM-style play to sneakily steal the Level 3 POS data that retailers don't want to give away (but that's essentially what it is!). The idea is that, say, Barclays add Itemize to their mobile banking app so that I scan my receipts into it and Barclays can then send me offers and other propositions based on knowing what I buy.

---

[25] *http://www.mobileworldlive.com/facebook-plans-mobile-money-service*
[26] *http://www.ft.com/cms/s/0/0e0ef050-c16a-11e3-97b2-00144feabdc0.html*

The Tomorrow's Transactions Reader 2015

I won't patronise you with all the cliches about how hard it was to choose a winner, and nor will I admit daylight to the judge's discussions, but in the end we choose Azimo. With an endorsement like that, it was only a matter of time before Facebook, Apple or Google came knocking on their door...

Bots and pluggers (15th May)

Had a conversation yesterday with someone about a new startup. I hope they won't mind me mentioning that one element of the conversation was about determining whether social media accounts were "real" or not. This reminded me what Sherry Turkle from MIT (who wrote the brilliant, seminal book on online identity, "Life on Screen") said last year, when talking about the specific issue of twitter bots and fake social media accounts, that this is a really serious and really important problem because of the inability to distinguish between real and fake accounts...

...will and should undermine trust

[From Twitter, Bots And Fake Accounts - Business Insider][27]

Indeed. I went to a marvellous panel session about this at SXSW, and I wrote at the time that there was a need to prove **what** you are (e.g., human) that is entirely distinct from the need to prove **who** you are:

An internet passport should be something different: whereas a mundane passport is valuable because it proves who you are, an internet passport should be valuable precisely because it doesn't.

[From In cyberspace, no-one knows you're a dogbot - Tomorrow's Transactions][28]

Given that the industrial-scale manufacturing of fake social media accounts is already widespread, you might wonder exactly who the fake accounts are for? I found this example in the WSJ quite interesting.

Rapper Tony Benson says hiring Mr. Vidmar to promote his account on Twitter is "the best decision I ever made." Mr. Vidmar's robots made the rapper, known as Philly Chase, a trending topic so often around Philadelphia that he attracted

---

[27] *http://www.businessinsider.com/twitter-bots-and-fake-accounts-2013-11#ixzz2lgJdFxjO*
[28] *http://tomorrowstransactions.com/2012/08/in-cyberspace-no-one-knows-youre-a-dogbot/*

attention from local newspapers. Prominence on Twitter led to gigs, fans and ways to promote his videos, Mr. Benson says.

[From Inside a Twitter Robot Factory - WSJ.com][29]

In the early days of the pop business, as it was then called, record companies used to employ "pluggers". In those days, the pop charts were compiled from the sales records of a small number of record shops. The identity of the shops was supposed to be secret, but the record companies of course knew which ones they were. So they would send their pluggers to buy copies of their own records to push their artists up the charts. Good for Tony Benson, who has found a way to replace pluggers with plugbots.

Much modern spam isn't designed for consumption by humans at all; instead, it's "robot-readable", created by one non-human entity for the attention of another – specifically, the "spiders" that crawl the web compiling data for Google – in the hope of pushing a junk page higher up the list of search results.

[From Why Spam Works - Business Insider][30]

Is Twitter becoming a vast network of bots talking to other bots? What a fascinating idea to play with, and what a wonderful proto-case study for the future of business. I stand by my prediction of long ago. One day, IS_A_PERSON may be the most valuable online credential of all.

Identity is, so I hear, the new money (12th June)

The wonderful people at the Centre for the Study of Financial Innovation (CSFI) in London did me the great honour of holding one of their super lunchtime roundtable meetings around the publication of my new book, *Identity is the New Money*. I gave a short talk on a couple of themes on the topic, starting by exploring Jack Weatherford's meme about the future of money being more like the money of the neolithic past than the money of today and finishing with the three suggestions for UK policy makers that I finished the book with — and trying to justify them to a financial services audience which, judging from some of the questions, I didn't do too badly at.

We need to begin by finding a way to make the construction and use of a new infrastructure for identity a national project of significance. We need

---

[29]

http://online.wsj.com/news/articles/SB10001424052702304607104579212122084821400

[30] http://www.businessinsider.com/why-spam-works-2013-8

to find something that can provide the "parasitic vitality" for a new identity paradigm. We already know that in the UK, as well as in the USA, Australia and many other countries, there is no appetite for any kind of national identity scheme. But there may be an alternative formulation that helps all stakeholders: individuals, business, governments, law enforcement and everyone else. A **National Entitlement Scheme**. Long before the late and unlamented national identity scheme in the UK, there was (back in 2002) the original proposal for an entitlement card. This should be revisited in the light of modern technology. We can use the modern privacy-enhancing infrastructure to decouple these entitlements from the underlying identities and resolve the paradox of more security and privacy.

One very specific use of the new infrastructure should be to greatly reduce the cost and complexity of executing transactions in the UK by explicitly recognising that reputation will be the basis of trust and therefore transaction costs. The regulators should therefore set in motion plans for a **Financial Services Passport**. This would use the same infrastructure as the National Entitlement Scheme but with a sector-specific profile. The UK's IT industry trade association, TechUK, has a working group looking at just this idea already and together with colleagues at Consult Hyperion we have put forward the same suggestion to the Federal Reserve in response to their November 2013 consultation on the evolution of the US Payments System. Since the financial services passport would be using the same infrastructure as the entitlesment scheme, one might expect the costs to be manageable and then cost savings to UK plc significant.

Finally, I should like to make a rather technical and boring plea to the relevant authorities to make the UK's **National Payments Plan** adopt an explicit target for reducing the total social cost of payments in the UK. This will inevitably mean coming up with tactics to reduce cash (and cheque) usage in the UK. This target will be made significantly easier to attain using the Financial Services Passport to lower the barriers to entry for new products and services, increasing competition in the sector (especially with respect to the financially-excluded groups who are too expensive to serve using existing infrastructure).

These are straightforward calls to action and I trust that you have been persuaded to support them!

I won't report the excellent and wide-ranging roundtable discussion that followed (which was held under the Chatham House rule) except to note that David Rennie -- from the Identity Assurance Programme (IDA) in the Government Digital Service (GDS) -- was kind enough to join me at the roundtable and talk about the government's current initiatives and how they support the idea of shifting toward entitlement as the basis for transactional interaction.

As is the tradition at such events, my publishers were kind enough to show up in person with a job lot of the heroic tome (plus some other titles in the Perspectives series) to knock out at the back and, despite accepting Bitcoin, Pingit, Paym and PayPal, I'm sorry to say that every single person who bought a copy paid cash. I will never recover from the shame.

P.S. Available at all good bookstores and some of the bad ones too. Kindle version now available as well. For our US readers, you can buy right now online with free shipping to the US[31]

---

[31] *http://bit.ly/1pdzFN0*

Chapter 3: Legal and Regulatory

It's crazy to talk about the online world as a lawless or a kind of Wild West when it simply isn't. Far from it. It is the regulatory framework for electronic transactions that, ultimately, determines the path of new entrants. It may be frustrating at times, but the onus is on technologists to try and inform regulators, to demonstrate the advantages of competition and free invention and to help to create a platform for innovation.

Bitcoin regulation–Don't Panic (18th March)

The regulation of Bitcoin should be about the principles of something rather than the specific nature of the technology used, but without talking to a lawyer at length it is not immediately obvious to me what those principles might be. Supposing that there is something like a blockchain where the ownership of a digital asset is established by "the community" in some way, then what regulation is needed? The digital asset in the distributed public ledger is "owned" by a public key. Anyone or everyone with the corresponding private key can do what they like with it. No private key, no can do. If I steal your private key, say, and transfer away a digital asset that you control, then that will be fraud (or whatever, please don't email me about this if it turns out that it is actually some other form of specific criminal activity) and that is already illegal. This seems to me the essence of the discussions about smart contracts and cryptocurrency scripting that are closer to the heart of the future cryptocurrency landscape than the Bitcoin currency today is. If you have the cryptography, if you have the scripting, and if you have the smart contracts that they create, then what you need regulation for?

As far as the means of exchange (ie, retail payments) is concerned, I don't see an issue. Overstock.com can accept anything they like as payment. They can take Bitcoins, soya beans or pork belly futures: it is up to them and their customers. I've written before that I think there is something of a misunderstanding about what Anglo-Saxon legal tender laws mean and imply. If you are a merchant and I am a customer, it's a matter of private contract between us as to how I might pay. Obviously we can't form private contracts that break the law, so we can't decide that I will pay using sex slaves or Ketamine, but you get my point. I'm sure somewhere in the Canon of US Federal and State Laws there are statutes concerning what **the** currency is, but I wonder if there's any such statutes concerning what **a** currency is? If there are, I'm genuinely interested to hear from people that know about this topic, as I'm pretty sure they wouldn't include Bitcoin. This is why I don't really understand the story about Californian legislators AB-129 "Lawful Money" bill.

"This bill makes clarifying changes to current law to ensure that various forms of alternative currency such as digital currency, points, coupons, or other objects of monetary value do not violate the law when those methods are used for the purchase of goods and services or the transmission of payments."

[From Californa Bill to Legalize Bitcoin and Alternative Currencies][32]

So it's against the law to pay people using Amazon vouchers? I doubt it. I'll have get back on to the lawyers to explain all of this me again, since I've no idea what this bill is for. If you and I agree to swap Bitcoins, Marks & Spencer's vouchers or old copies of The Daily Telegraph for lawnmowers, train tickets or cups of coffee, it's up to us. There's no law that says that I have to accept US Dollars or Visa cards or cheques.

As was observed in the discussion of the Snap Cafe, you cannot force a retailer to accept cash. If, however, you buy something from them and there is no contractual barrier to the use of cash, and you offer legal tender in payment, and they refuse it, then they cannot enforce the debt in court.

[From Payment and tender - Tomorrow's Transactions][33]

This is not to say that no regulation at all is required. In Mark Hochstein's brilliant cover story on Bitcoin in American Banker he makes the point that exchanges (the in/out points for fiat currency) are a special case. If I am going to convert cash into Bitcoins or Bitcoins into cash, that's a business that needs to be regulated. But it already is.

For many bankers, guidance released last year by the Treasury Department's Financial Crimes Enforcement Network, which subjected virtual currency firms to the same know-your-customer requirements as traditional money services businesses, hasn't sufficed to remove the scarlet "A" (for anonymity) from these startups.

[From Why Bitcoin Matters for Bankers - American Banker Magazine Article][34]

---

[32] *http://bitcoinmagazine.com/10159/california-bill-legalize-bitcoin/*

[33] *http://tomorrowstransactions.com/2007/10/payment-and-ten/#more-1416*
[34] *http://www.americanbanker.com/magazine/124_02/why-bitcoin-matters-for-bankers-1065590-1.html*

This seems to be an appropriate general approach and it isn't a surprise to see other jurisdictions adopting the same approach, most recently Singapore, for example.

The Monetary Authority of Singapore will require intermediaries that facilitate the exchange of digital currencies to verify customers' identities and report suspicious transactions to a unit of the city-state's police

[From Singapore to Regulate Bitcoin Operators for Laundering Risk - Bloomberg]

I might have my own opinions on the extent to which the Financial Action Task Force (FATF) guidelines should be applied (broadly speaking I'm in favour of relaxing controls at the low-end and toughening controls at the high-end, as the FATF recommend in their risk-based approach) but I can see that the principle of this regulation makes sense. But regulating whether consumers can or cannot use Bitcoins to buy things or not doesn't fit. Therefore, when comparing regulatory environments and trying to work out which might be appropriate, I would have thought that Bitcoin was more of a form of barter than anything else and, as it happens, the Bank of England agree with me.

As such they may have more conceptual similarities to commodities, such as gold, than money

[From Bank of England: Digital Currencies are Similar to Commodities]

Maybe the lawyers can tell us whether there is appropriate regulation that can be extended to the digital world, and I'd be interested to hear about it, but I really don't think we should be panicked into emergency regulations about Bitcoins at all.

Payment system regulation as barrier to payment system innovation (16ᵗʰ June)

There was a good article back in the September *Financial World* magazine arguing that transparency is a key to regaining confidence in the banking system. I agree strongly, and I'm not the only one.

More transparent record keeping would allow law enforcement to trace the transfer of funds and identify those responsible for the illicit use or theft of virtual currency.

[From Virtual Currencies, Real Theft - Javelin Strategy & Research Blog][35]

Indeed it would, and some might argue that that transparency be extended to legacy infrastructure as well. (It's not really the topic of this post but remember than transparency need not subvert privacy. You could have pseudonymous dark pools but force the release of linked identities given a warrant, for example.) If, however, transparency is taken to mean thorough KYC/AML/ATF procedures (henceforth known as CDD, or customer due diligence) that identify all participants to a transaction to all observers, then it will force criminals, terrorists and corrupt politicians to abandon electronic means of exchange and go back to cash. If that happens, then we are all worse off. Having some traceability is better than having none at all, as I've argued before. And it's not as if having rigorous CDD solves the problem.

Worse still, the increased cost associated with a tougher stance on KYC does nothing to make the system any more secure, and may in fact drive up risk rather than reduce it.

[From Cost of KYC too high says Swiss start up » Banking Technology][36]

I suppose you could argue that what is driving the players at the moment is not risk but liability. So long as they can shift the liability onto someone else, no-one really cares who you are. The system is broken.

The two set up 68 accounts in 19 different cities using 24 aliases to handle the transfer of funds and sent the bulk of the money to individuals in Nigeria, who set up the operation. Money was also wired to addresses in the UK, Ecuador, India, the United Arab Emirates, and the US, none of which has been recovered.

[From Mother/daughter team jailed for million-dollar internet dating scam • The Register][37]

Hold on. 68 accounts using 24 aliases? What was the point of the billions of dollars spent on KYC, AML and ATF? And why am I going on about this anyway? Well, in her keynote at Payments Innovation 2014, Mary Starks (the acting MD for the UK's new Payment System Regulator) said

---

[35] *https://www.javelinstrategy.com/blog/2012/09/13/virtual-currencies-real-theft/*
[36] *http://www.bankingtech.com/195632/cost-of-kyc-too-high-says-swiss-start-up*
[37]

http://www.theregister.co.uk/2013/08/30/motherdaughter_team_jailed_for_milliondollar_internet_dating_scam/

---

that on the whole regulators "don't do innovation". I was on the panel with her, so I made what I think was a reasonable point that the best regulatory approach to innovation is competition, and that a focus on reducing the barriers to entry to payments markets that do not involve systemic risk is probably sufficient. We don't need to imagine what people might come up with, we just want to make it easy for them to do so.

When it came to the discussion that followed, I used CDD as an example of such a barrier. The costs and complexity of CDD can make it very difficult for new entrants, especially those dealing with low-value payments, the excluded and specialist niches to get off the ground. One of the reasons for this is that there is no infrastructure for them to plug in to, so everyone has to build everything from scratch.

Surely all of this dialogue about passports and utility bills, declarations and signatories and KYC and AML is pushing a demand for a new digital infrastructure to cure all of this mess.

[From Digital identities demand a digital infrastructure | Banking View][38]

Karen Wendel from Identrust talked about the infrastructural approach in her presentation as well, and this all links to the discussions about the idea of a financial service passport (or a "pay name") at techUK last year. I really think that the idea of pseudonymous, strongly-authenticated CDD-inside identities is an idea whose time has come. I should be able to participate in a transaction as John Doe, provided that I can prove that someone (e.g., my bank) knows who John Doe actually is and that is is someone who has been approved after CDD. You don't need to know who I am to do business with me, so long as you know that **someone** knows who I am..

The phantom NEELIE (the missing third scheme) (3ʳᵈ July)

In the winter 2013/2014 Journal of Payments Strategy & Systems (Vol. 7, No. 4, p. 344-358) there is an excellent paper by Ewald Judt and Malte Krueger called *A European card payments scheme: forever a phantom?* which is about the European so-called "third scheme", otherwise known as the European Card Payment Scheme (ECPS), otherwise known (by me) as the EU Non-American Emergent Electronic Legacy Interchange Exclusion scheme, or the NEELIE for short.

The authors set out to try to understand why generations of European policymakers have failed to create a pan-European alternative to (in

---

[38] *http://blogs.sap.com/banking/2014/03/13/digital-identities-demand-a-digital-infrastructure/*

essence) Visa and MasterCard and conclude that (and I paraphrase) that there are three main reasons:

- There are genuine economies of scale.

- The historical timing of the MasterCard IPO and competition authorities pressure on interchange means that the opportunity has passed.

- Bank management doesn't care.

I think that this last point is important for policymakers to fully understand. Banks are not that bothered by the current situation, as it kind of suits them. Now, when it comes to competition policy and interchange rates I have constantly argued for competition rather than regulation in the sector. Policymakers should focus on competition in the payment sector – which Europe, to be fair, has done to some extent – and let the market work out interchange rates for itself.

Forcing banks to create a third scheme with low interchange rates just isn't going to work. And it's looking in the rear-view mirror anyway. If the European Commission wants to create a dynamic new payment service across Europe, why would it bother with cards at all? Why not a euro M-PESA, setting to one side the fact that the Commission is (as I understand it) going to rule against using M-PESA accounts in Romania as "euro basic bank accounts" under impending regulation. I don't get it.

The authors point out the contradictions between, broadly speaking, using competition policy or regulation to obtain the Commission's desired outcome. There is a tension that will need to be resolved at the policy level, because competition (my preferred solution) will not deliver what they want. I think this is a good thing, personally. I also think that the mental model behind this (that there should be a card that can be used at any terminal in Europe) is somewhat last century. Having 50 different cards in my wallet that I need to use in different places in Europe would, of course, be a real pain in the arse. But having 50 different apps on my phone? Not a problem: especially since the phone knows where I am so it can use an appropriate payment mechanism wherever I am and link all of them (via the proposed euro-API for banking) back to my account automatically so it doesn't need to bother me about that sort of thing at all.

Celent does not believe that any of the main contenders will deliver a new viable and competitive European card scheme any time soon. Furthermore, we argue that the market has moved on in the last seven years, and the case for a European-only card scheme created from scratch is simply no longer there, if it ever was.

[From In Search of a Third European Card Scheme: Time to Move On | Celent][39]

Indeed. And that was written a couple of years ago. If we ever do build the NEELIE, it will be for political purposes, a sort of symbolic pan-European canal network in the age of the bullet train. Why bother?

Didn't we have a lovely day, the day we went to the Italian Parliament (29th July)

I went off to Italy to take part in a hearing about Bitcoin in the Italian Parliament. Naturally, the hard work began the night before with a delicious meal in the centre of Rome. It's important to soak up the atmosphere before speaking in a parliament building I always feel.

I had dinner with Jordan Kelly. Jordan is the CEO of Robocoin, who are launching a network of Bitcoin ATMs. We found a lot to share in our world views, even though we don't agree about everything. Which was good, because it was important to put a spectrum of views in front of the hearing. Next morning, we set off for the Italian Parliament building, Montecitorio, for the public hearing. The nice people at Cashless Way made a photo album of the day for you[40,] by the way.

Our host was Geronimo Emili (below) from the "War on Cash", who had invited Jordan and I as the overseas "experts", joining the list of Italian individuals and organisations speaking at the event. These included MasterCard, Unicredit, the consumer association, acdemics, entrepreneurs and the tax police. A fascinating, fascinating range of views. I won't regurgitate here because the discussions have been covered elsewhere but I focused my contribution on the radical and innovative nature of the Bitcoin protocol while remaining sceptical about the potential for Bitcoin as a currency (although I did support the idea that new kinds of currency are around the corner).

In preparation for the day's activities, I created a new Bitcoin Wallet and posted it to Twitter to appeal for donations to try out the new Bitcoin ATM later on. And guess what! A kind soul sent a donation! Under the cloak of anonymity and with an increase in the sum total of human knowledge as their only reward, a benefactor responded.

After the presentations in the parliament, we all went over to the LUISS EnLabs accelerator where the Robocoin Bitcoin ATM was duly unveiled

---

[39] *http://celent.com/reports/search-third-european-card-scheme-time-move*
[40] *https://www.flickr.com/photos/cashlessway/sets/72157645142504369/*

to appropriate media fanfare and members of the general public (sort of) were invited to give it a go.

So here's how it works. You register with the network. You enter your mobile phone number. The system texts you a code. You enter the code. Then you hold your ID (in my case, a passport) up to the scanner and then you place your right hand it a palm scanner (four times). The you look in the camera and it takes your picture so the person at the other end of the line (it is a person) can see that you are the person in the ID document. You log in. You generate a Bitcoin Wallet.

And then you wait. You get a text message when the chap at the other end has OK'd everything. When you get confirmation that your account has been created, you put money into the ATM, it credits the cash to the wallet. Alternatively, you can turn Bitcoins in the wallet into cash. So, you log in to your account and then you feed money into the slot. Once this is done, the ATM prints out a ticket for you with the wallet private key on it. You can hide this under your bed, have it tattooed on your inner thigh or, as I did, "sweep" it into another wallet.

I gave it a go. My €50 was determined to be real, presumably, and the system generated a receipt for the transaction. And then the blockchain goes off and does its stuff and some indeterminate time later, the purchased Bitcoins show up in your wallet.

Did it work? Yes it did. Was it easy and convenient? No it wasn't. Will the general public use it? I wouldn't have thought so, although it may well find a niche. Personally, I can't really imagine any circumstances under which I'd use it, and there are two main reasons for this.

The first is that I already have a bank account that works fine and I'd rather people who want to give me money just send it to my bank account so I don't have to go near an ATM anyway.

The second is the pain of KYC. I gave my passport details, mobile phone number and palm print to a box of unknown provenance (well, not strictly true, since I'd met Jordan and he's nice guy) and I was distinctly uncomfortable about it. And all the time I was doing it I was wondering why. It's just not worth the hassle or the risk.

So, in summary, I stand by my comments to the hearing. Bitcoin is a genuine technological breakthrough and it will cause a revolution. But probably not in payments.

The Tomorrow's Transactions Reader 2015

It is meaningless to say that the British government will "legalise" Bitcoin. Oh, and wrong, too (14th August)

Britain's Minister of Finance, a man of the people who for historical reasons is known as George Gideon Oliver Osborne, of the Baronetcy of Ballentaylor and Ballylemon in the County of Waterford, Chancellor of the Exchequer and Second Lord of the Treasury, gave a speech at the Innovate Finance conference in London, in which he said that he had instructed Treasury officials to work on a study (ie, hire one of the usual management consultancies to knock up a study) looking at the benefits and threats of digital currencies, although he didn't say the benefits to whom or the threats from what. Rather bizarrely, this was reported as (in The Telegraph, for example[41]) "Chancellor embraces Bitcoin". Strange. A more accurate headline, I'm sure, would be "Chancellor has only a faint notion of what Bitcoin is and, frankly, doesn't really care". I even saw one or two comments along the lines of "British government may legalise Bitcoin", which set me thinking...

Bitcoin is a decentralized, unregulated virtual currency now used by some 100,000 merchants worldwide. It is not legal tender in most countries.

[From Irish Central Banker Lays Down the Law at Bitcoin Gathering - Digits - WSJ][42]

It is not, as far as I know, legal tender in **any** country. Nor, I would wager, will it **ever** be. Legal tender is an outdated and essentially meaningless concept, which is why I am baffled by the reporting around the topic. And the regulation of cryptocurrency in general. To pick one example, having asked a few different experts, I'm none the wiser as to what it means to say that California has "legalised Bitcoin" or anything like it and would welcome clarification from experts in the field.

"Existing law prohibits a corporation, flexible purpose corporation, association, or individual from issuing or putting in circulation, as money, anything but the lawful money of the United States,"

[From California legalizes bitcoin - San Francisco Business Times][43]

---

[41] *http://www.telegraph.co.uk/finance/currency/11014508/George-Osborne-embraces-Bitcoin-as-London-aims-to-be-centre-of-global-financial-technology-revolution.html*
[42] *http://blogs.wsj.com/digits/2014/07/03/irish-central-banker-lays-down-the-law-at-bitcoin-gathering/*

Precisely how the new law from <u>Governor Moonbeam</u> (which is what he was called when I used to live in California) is going to change anything is entirely opaque to me. Businesses were free to accept Bitcoin in payment as a matter of private contract. What you couldn't do is **force** a business to accept Bitcoin, and you still can't. But then, you can't force a business to accept US dollars either, as I mentioned here <u>eight years ago</u>[44]. So what was the barrier that was torn down in California?

According to the report "governments should consider eliminating any and all regulatory or legal obstacles to the use of private monies".

[From <u>Ditch legal tender to unleash bitcoin - think tank</u>]

All regulatory obstacles? Really? I don't want to transact in the dark! I don't think we should eliminate all regulatory obstacles: I don't want to live an electronic Somalia. But when it comes to money, it seems to me that the obstacles are minimal (pretty much anyone can get an Electronic Money Issuer licence in the EU right now) and it has nothing to do with "legal tender" at all.

Several countries - including US and Germany - have declared that bitcoin is not a currency but property for tax purposes.

[From <u>Ditch legal tender to unleash bitcoin - think tank</u>][45]

And I agree with this too. Bitcoin is property, not currency. End of. I don't see why this is in the least bit controversial and I'm surprised that Baronet Osborne didn't ask me about it, but if his management consultants want a word, I'll be back in the office on Monday.

What exactly is "appropriate" AML? (1ˢᵗ December)

In his first major speech, the new European Commissioner for Financial Stability, Financial Services and Capital Markets, Jonathan Hill, talked (amongst other things) about innovation in digital money and virtual currencies, saying that:

---

[43] *http://www.bizjournals.com/sanfrancisco/morning_call/2014/06/california-legalizes-bitcoin-jerry-brown-ab-129.html*

[44] *http://tomorrowtransactions.com/2006/11/snap/*

[45] *http://www.finextra.com/news/fullstory.aspx?newsitemid=26179*

The Tomorrow's Transactions Reader 2015

when considering electronic financial services, we need to strike the appropriate balance between guarding against fraud, hackers and money laundering and maintaining ease of use for customers.

[From Turning around the telescope – consumers at the centre of financial services policies][46]

He is right about this, of course, but I wonder what the benchmark for determining what is "appropriate" is? I don't think we should cripple the development of digital money by applying benchmarks that are so stringent, so rigorous, so absurd that they stop progress completely. We should be building digital money systems that are better than cash, yes, but to pick on one of the Commissioner's specific points, we should not be applying utterly inappropriate, expensive and pointless anti-money laundering (AML) rules, especially when Europe as a whole is doing nothing about cash.

I noticed this in a story in *The Times* (21st August 2014). The story is headlined "Playboy Saudi prince 'blackmailed' after Paris ambush" and concerns the theft of £400,000 in cash from a 12 car convoy taking the entourage of the prince to Le Bourget airport. (The newspaper reports that, in a plot worthy of a John Grisham novel, the theft of the cash may have been a cover for the theft of documents containing sensitive information.) Now, if you or I were to carry more than €4,700 into or out of France, we would have to declare it to customs. However at Le Bourget, as *The Times* puts it, such controls are not "strictly" applied. For those without private planes, though, the cross-border payments infrastructure is less facilitating.

In addition, money-laundering regulations are putting impossible demands on systems designed to serve the poor, requiring, for instance, "know your customer" procedures like taking copies of ID documents for anyone receiving an international payout.

[From Remittance rip-offs - WorldNews][47]

So you can't help but wonder what the point of stringent KYC/AML/ATF controls over people sending part of their meagre paycheque from the UK back to Somalia or from South Africa back to DRC are, when rich people with private planes can import and export unlimited amounts of untraceable cash? The impact of such controls, as far as I can see, is twofold: firstly, criminals and terrorists use cash so we can't monitor their activities and, secondly, the costs of sending money are higher than they should otherwise be.

---

[46] http://europa.eu/rapid/press-release_SPEECH-14-1905_en.htm
[47] http://article.wn.com/view/2014/04/22/Remittance_ripoffs/

43

Africa pays a "remittance supertax" of nearly $2bn a year due to the higher-than-average cost of sending money to the continent, according to... The Overseas Development Institute,

[From Africans face $2bn yearly 'remittance supertax', FT][48]

Average remittance fees for sending money to Africa are around 12% (as opposed to the global average of 8% and the UN target of 5%). And remember, these fees fall on people sending money home to their families.

The biggest challenge for the MSB sector is adapting and responding to the global banking de-risking agenda, which is threatening the development and recovery in emerging economies and post-conflict states around the world.

[From Operating in conflict zones: lessons from a financial institution in Somalia | The Guardian]

Now, it's not as if the powers that be do not know about this problem. The international body that is charged with reviewing such things is the Financial Action Task Force (FATF) and in their February 2013 paper on *Anti-Money Laundering and Terrorist Financing Measures and Financial Inclusion* [PDF] they themselves point out that overly prescriptive legislation can cause payment organisations to be so risk-averse that millions of people are excluded from global remittances. And, as Consult Hyperion has noted in its work for the UK government in this area, payments organisations are wary of offering services even when they think they comply with such overly prescriptive legislation because of their worries about future turns of events. As Neil Burton, who knows a thing or two about international payments, wrote earlier this year:

Easily said, but less easily resolved, when fines are in excess of $1bn, and the right to operate in the US is at risk.

[From INTERNATIONAL PAYMENTS COMPLIANCE: SEEKING CERTAINTY AMID COMPLEXITY][49]

Surely there is something fundamentally wrong with a set of legislative arrangements that mean that the rich can ship money around freely but the poor have to pay 12% to transfer tiny amounts. The current system cannot be "appropriate" whichever way you look at it..

---

[48] http://www.ft.com/cms/s/0/2c1451ce-c4b9-11e3-9aeb-00144feabdc0.html?siteedition=intl#axzz2zBS5NJRC
[49] http://www.globalbankingandfinance.com/international-payments-compliance-seeking-certainty-amid-complexity/

Part 2: Money
Chapter 4: History and Future

I am convinced that the best way to understand the future of transactions is to understand their past. The complex inter-relationship between social, business and technology developments means that it is very difficult to imagine the impact of new technologies in the transaction space. But we can look back, to examine disruptive (and unexpected) consequences of previous technology revolutions and use them to imagine plausible futures for individuals, businesses and governments.

Speed is just a question of money, except when it comes to payments (9th April)

The US Postal Service launched its New York to Chicago service in September 1919 but it was often interrupted by bad weather and so letters continued to go by rail. In 1925 a group of Chicago bankers petitioned for a more reliable service on the grounds that if they could fly checks overnight between Chicago and New York instead of sending them by rail, then they would clear a day sooner giving the banks quicker access to the money. They were quite prepared to pay a premium for such a service.

The solution seems to me astonishing, but it happened. As Hiawatha Bray explains in his excellent book on the history of navigation, You Are Here, the Post Office was building a series of 50 foot tall towers, three miles apart, to provide gas-powered flames capable of guiding planes over long distances. So they built a series of towers all the way between Chicago and New York and the mail could be carried overnight and the banks cheerfully (well, I've no idea whether they were cheerful or not) paid a premium in the region of four times the rate the standard mail. That Chicago-New York route continues to drive innovation today.

No wonder that Spread Networks, the company building the fibre-optic connection, proudly boasted: "Round-trip travel time from Chicago to New Jersey has been cut to 13 milliseconds."

And HFTs were willing to pay through the nose to use it, with the first 200 to sign up forking out $2.8bn between them.

[From High-frequency trading: when milliseconds mean millions - Yahoo Finance UK][50]

That was then. This is now and, because as you can imagine, 13 milliseconds is to just far too long for data to get between the major financial markets in Chicago and New York, money is driving further development.

One new hot market for microwave providers is between New York and Chicago, both cities with many financial services firms... Based on the speed of light, the theoretical limit for sending information between New York and Chicago is 7.96 milliseconds. Right now, the state-of-the-art among microwave service providers is about 8.5 milliseconds,

[From Microwave vies with fiber for high-frequency trading - Computerworld]

So, right now, folk are investing in communication links that will cut 4.5 milliseconds from the time it takes to send information between the markets. Pathetic! There's still a further 540 nanoseconds to go, you sluggards! A lot can happen in 540 nanoseconds! The speed of modern communications is astonishing. You can send financial services data at almost the speed of light. Incredible.

Meanwhile, in Episode #489 NPR's Planet Money, I hear "We just need Amazon's bank to send money electronically to a checking account at Chase bank. It's just information traveling over wires. How long could it take: A minute? An hour? It took five days". That's longer than it took to send money between Chicago and New York in 1925, before the airmail service launched.

London money soon please (8th May)

I happened to be reading the Havas "14 trends for 2014" by Marian Salzman[51] and noted with interest her point about post-nationalism, countries breaking up and London becoming independent from the UK. I'm sure some of the people reading this thought it a little far-fetched, but I don't. A long time ago, I read a book by the Canadian author Jane Jacobs. It was called "Cities and the Wealth of Nations". It was of those books that you come across now and then that makes you change your world view as soon as you start reading it, because you immediately recognise that the

---

[50] *https://uk.finance.yahoo.com/news/high-frequency-trading-milliseconds-mean-234410364.html*
[51] *http://havaspr.com/us/?page_id=3081*

author's perspective is correct. Jane's book definitely had that impact on me, and it made me see the dominance of London and its hinterland in a different light.

You may wonder why I'm bringing up the issue of cities and their hinterlands now. Well, I've brought it up before, and so have other people in the context of thinking about the future of money. Remember, for example, Gill Ringland's work on "Long Finance" scenarios for 2050? — *In Safe Hands? The Future of Financial Services.* SAMI (Dec. 2011).

Having listened to Gill and the audience response to her scenarios, I'm more convinced than ever that the world of the "C50" (the organisation of the 50 richest city-states that will replace the G20 as the mechanism for "managing" the world economy) which comes from her "Many Hands" scenario, will be the most likely basis for the future economic organisation of a successful, functional world.

[From Search for "gill ringland" - Tomorrow's Transactions]

Gill said that in this scenario, cities might become the source of money and identity, the two things that interest me most and the platform for almost all of Consult Hyperion's customers' businesses, so I asked her along to our 2012 Forum and she gave a terrific presentation. I'm sure many in the audience saw her ideas as being somewhat speculative, just like Marian's, and I suppose that may have been understandable. Well, understandable, until it was written over at the Financial Times that:

To make wise decisions, investors and policy makers need to view the world not so much as a collection of countries but a network of cities.

[From Cities, not countries, are the key to tomorrow's economies - FT.com]

Indeed. In my podcast with the brilliant Felix Martin (the author of *Money: An Unauthorised Biography* and keynote speaker at our 2014 Forum) he talks about the "bargain" around technology and money, the bargain between sovereign and business, the bargain that the late Professor Glyn Davies said (at the very first Consult Hyperion Forum) has always served to weaken the power of the sovereign. Felix talks about the Bank of England using something like Bitcoin to issue an electronic currency, Bank-of-England-coins or something like that. I discussed why this might be a good idea recently. But suppose we combine these two sets of ideas and argue for electronic currency issued not by countries, but by cities or regions? Now in the podcast, Felix sensibly attempts to refute some of my crackpot theories about London having its own money and Scotland launching the first wholly virtual fiat currency, but I feel that the tectonic plates underlying currency have shifted in my direction. Once again, let's pop over to the Financial Times to see what the great and good are thinking, as distinct from wide-eyed techno-determinists like me.

> *"London is far richer [than Scotland], and could easily be fiscally self-sufficient. It is the nation's cash cow. This is the age of cities, not of national economies. It is high time London became a true city state."*

> *[From Capital gains fuel visions of a breakaway London - FT.com]*

How true this is. And the right place to start would be to stop London from distorting the UK economy further by making it have its own money. We already have two economies in the UK — London and everywhere else — so we should recognise that and take London out of the Sterling Zone as soon as possible!

McPESA (29th April)

I'll be heading up to the Financial Service Club in Edinburgh tonight to give a talk on Scottish independence, digital money and freedom! As I wrote in my blog piece yesterday, which was an online version of an article published 13 years ago, it is time for Scotland to drive a technological stake into the high ground and become the world's first electronic currency state! In case you think I'm a nutter (which is, at best, unproven), or at least a blinkered technological determinist only interested in enriching Consult Hyperion clients in the electronic transactions space (which is true), I want to point out that I am not the only the person who thinks that its time for state e-currency, and it's interesting to see why (which isn't a love of technology).

> *Now, more than ever, is the time for central banks to launch their own official e-money.*

> *[From The time for official e-money is NOW! | FT Alphaville]*

Other than cost savings and convenience, you might wonder why economists think that electronic money is a good idea. Well, here's what Citi's chief economist has to say about it:

> *The purpose of the exercise is to eliminate a silly asymmetry in the monetary policy arsenal. Because of the existence of currency with a zero nominal interest rate, the interest nominal*

rate on all financial assets is constrained to be no lower than zero

[From The Wonderful World of Negative Nominal Interest Rates, Again | willem buiter's maverecon][52]

Why not have the new Scottish central bank seize the initiative? Just because we do things in a certain way doesn't make them laws of nature, especially where money is concerned. The use of commercial banks to create money was a limitation of the technology of the day: the use of the payment technology of the day to create sovereign money was a bargain between the commercial banks and the sovereign that made sense in days of yore. But as the Positive Money people point out in their pamphlet on designing a Scottish currency, there is no obvious reason for a newly independent Scotland to go down that path.

So we should contemplate the re-emergence of the Scots pound; my own preference is to restore the groat or the bawbee. With its own currency, Scotland could pursue independent economic policies as economic realities and EU obligations would allow.

[From John Kay - Currency unknowns weigh on an independent Scotland][53]

Forgot about the political or narrative reasons for doing this, it makes sense in economic terms. Remember John Major's splendid idea for the hard ECU? It is entirely possible to imagine a new currency that is designed to exist solely in electronic form and there are many advantages to doing so.

This option would see the creation of a new currency entirely disconnected from any other currency.

[From What currency should an independent Scotland adopt?| Scots Independence News | The Week UK]

A "hard e-thistle" would be a new currency, under the control of a Scottish central bank, that would only ever exist in electronic form. Scottish shops would naturally accept it and they would mark prices in e-thistles, but they could also accept Sterling and Euros in note and coin form if they want to continue to accept cash. I'm sure a great many wouldn't bother.

---

[52] *http://blogs.ft.com/maverecon/2009/05/the-wonderful-world-of-negative-nominal-interest-rates-again/#axzz30AZjqPUX*
[53] *http://www.johnkay.com/2014/02/26/currency-unknowns-weigh-on-an-independent-scotland*

I am not myself a Scottish nationalist, but if I were I would want my country to have its own currency.

[From <u>Scotland and currencies</u>][54]

There's the potential for a terrific national narrative around this. It would position Scotland as a modern economy, thought leaders and free thinkers, in the vanguard of the new monetary order. Whether they decided to use MintChip or Mondex, Bitcoin or McPESA they would be signalling a lot more than reduced costs for retail businesses.

I have a particular interest in the history of Scottish banks because of the lessons of that period of "free banking". This does not, as you might think, mean that Scottish banks were once operated as charities but that they were free to compete in note issue. And the result, as most historians would confirm, was a period of incredible innovation when the more tightly regulated London and country banks failed more often than the less tightly regulated Scottish banks did (I know this is an appalling precis of a complicated and interesting period, but I'm trying to make a bigger point).

[From <u>Digital Money: Freebanking and free banking</u>]

Scotland had an enviable track record of innovation in the finance and banking sector right up until the time when the Bank of England's outrageous monopoly was extended north of the border. When a previous wave of innovation (paper money) swept through the economy, Scotland was far more successful than England in exploiting technological change to make the economy more efficient (and more stable). **By 1850, in fact, when 90% of all commercial transactions in France were still being settled in gold or silver (as were a third of those in England), 90% of all commercial transactions in Scotland were being settled with paper**.

Surely it would be possible for Scotland to embrace the next wave of change in the technology of money (digital money) and generate yet more innovation. The regulatory environment is changing to encourage competition in Europe. The European Commission's Directive on Electronic Money, the Payment Services Directive (PSD and PSD2) have created the institutions — the Electronic Money Institutions (ELMI) and the Payment Institution (PI) to allow Scotland to start innovating now, never mind when it is independent in a couple of years!

But a variable exchange rate between Scots and English pounds would be a nuisance for individuals and business even if, as

---

[54] *http://johnredwoodsdiary.com/2014/01/30/scotland-and-currencies/*

would be likely, the rate did not fluctuate much. The queues at the bureau de change at Edinburgh's Waverley railway station would be the most visible manifestation,

[From John Kay - Currency unknowns weigh on an independent Scotland]

But would this be true with a hard e-thistle? There would be no queues at f/x bureaus because there would be **nothing to change the foreign currency into**: I suppose frequent travellers might obtain hard e-thistle prepaid cards, just like I have prepaid cards in Aussie dollars and Canuck loonies. But most of the time I just use my chip and PIN cards, my smart watch and my mobile phone to buy stuff. I didn't get any physical Aussie dollars last time I went there and I didn't get any physical Canuck loonies last time I went there either. Why would I bother with thistles?

There is no need for notes and coins (except as post-functional cash) and Consult Hyperion's experiences ranging from chip and PIN to M-PESA and from Mondex to MPOS can help the new Scottish government to design and build money for the 21st century while remembering the 19th!

Money that understands us (22nd April)

The 17th annual Tomorrow's Transactions Forum, held in London in March, was absolutely terrific. As always, I asked one of my very favourite writers, Wendy Grossman, to come along. I've been reading Wendy for many years, and her acute and accurate observations on the technology scene have always attracted my attention. Last time that Wendy was mentioned in dispatches from the Forum it was for offering to lick people's money, but this time I want to enter her into the Tomorrow's Transactions Chronicle because she came up with an astonishing turn of phrase that is proving impossible for me to to forget.

We are moving from money we understand to money that understands us.

[From net.wars: A money that understands us][55]

I was very taken with this brilliant encapsulation of a couple of thousand years of monetary evolution from coins made from precious metals to computations across the social graph. Identity is the new money as they

---

[55]

http://www.pelicancrossing.net/netwars/2014/03/a_money_that_understands_us.ht ml say. Well, as I say. To capture all of this in (and I mean this appreciatively, not dismissively) a T-shirt slogan is a breakthrough. I'm going to use this in literally every single presentation I give for the foreseeable future.

We no longer have money that we understand. Most people don't know how a credit card card works. The person in the street doesn't understand where money comes from or how it works. I know for a fact that some of them think that there is gold in the Bank of England that sits behind each banknote, something that hasn't been true for nearly a century. .

> *The general public don't really understand how it works and they don't really care.*

> *[From Search for "journalist gold bank of england" - Tomorrow's Transactions][56]*

We now have money that understands us. Barclays, Visa, MasterCard, Amex, Simple, Loop, Amazon - they all know what I bought yesterday, where I bought it, when I bought it, how often I bought it and so on.

> *New data visualization technology is now empowering banks to understand and capitalize on payment data that has historically been hidden away in inscrutable databases and spreadsheets.*

> *[From Visualizing Payments Data for Customer Analytics - BAI | Banking Strategies]*

Money that understands us. One of our clients was exploring some ideas around this recently: it wouldn't be appropriate to talk about the context, but one aspect of the business model is related to data that comes from electronic transactions, data that didn't exist in an era of non-electronic transactions but that businesses have not yet evolved to use effectively. There's going to be a lot of activity in this space over the next couple of years. Money that understands us. Brilliant: Wendy, I owe you one..

No need to guess the fintech future (23rd September)

The illuminated amongst us have long known that Dr. Who sends us secret coded messages that tell us about the future and so it is the most important television programme in the world for fintech folks. Therefore I was upset to see that the secret was out on Twitter.

> *All the #fintech people out there will love the fact the latest #DrWho episode had them robbing a bank :)*

---

[56] *http://tomorrowstransactions.com/?s=journalist+gold+bank+of+england*

The Tomorrow's Transactions Reader 2015

Kristoffer Lawson (@Setok) September 21, 2014

So now you know where I get my ideas. The truth is out there, as they say, if you know the URL. But then you already know that Dr. Who is where I get my ideas from.

> *When I said that I was genuinely surprised to find my talk on digital identity featured on TED, I meant it.*
>
> *From "You don't have to be psychic but it helps" at Tomorrow's Transactions[57]*

I'm not making this up. It's true. I'd picked up a number of ideas from my colleagues at Consult Hyperion and had assembled them into an identity ideas package to take to a few clients. I was looking around for a better non-technical narrative when I happened to be watching Dr. Who with my sons one day and… suddenly… it was all clear.

> *The variant I propose is to be known as Dr. Brown's psychic paper, named in honour of the Prime Minister who will scrap the current ID card scheme to universal acclaim and replace it with something fit for the 21st century (namely, this scheme). Unlike Dr. Who's psychic paper, Dr. Brown's psychic paper only shows the viewer what he or she wants to see if the holder has the relevant credential.*
>
> *From It's crazy, but it might just work at Tomorrow's Transactions[58]*

This turned out to be a wonderful, wonderful happenstance.

> *First of all, we all grew up with Dr. Who, so it engenders warm nostalgia. Now, obviously, there's an age-related component to this. My favourite monsters were the cybermen and I always wanted to be Brigadier-General Lethbridge-Stewart, so that gives my age away, but my kids look forward to it every week just as I did. Secondly, because the scriptwriters are skilled at engaging a non-technical audience we can piggyback on their imagery to interact with that same audience. And finally, because it's fun!*
>
> *From RUSI and all that at Tomorrow's Transactions[59]*

---

[57] *http://tomorrowstransactions.com/2012/07/you-dont-have-to-be-psychic-but-it-helps/*
[58] *http://tomorrowstransactions.com/2008/06/its-crazy-but-i/*
[59] *http://tomorrowstransactions.com/2008/07/rusi-and-all-th/*

When I used Dr. Who's psychic paper to explain how identity should work to support transactions in an online world, I think people really got it. I wrote a few papers and articles on the topic in which I also stressed that the "tap and go" convenience of NFC would be a way of making identity work for real. And then... Dr. Who got on a London bus (to Mars, which I think is the number 521 from Waterloo) using his psychic paper, thus demonstrating to the whole world that NFC is the future interface of choice.

This gave me the full package; so when I was asked to explain to banks or a telco or whoever what the future digital wallet should look like, I told that it was something like psychic paper.

Whatever description you chose, his Psychic Paper is exactly what a digital wallet should aspire to be

From <u>Dr. Who and the Psychic Paper -</u> at trishburgess.com

Indeed. Psychic paper (or the iPhone 7, as we call it) shows us everything we need to know about the future of financial transactions. It manages the individual's identity and displays the transaction-relevant attributes only to people authorised to see them. Everyone else sees nothing. Nothing at all.

"95% of fraud prevention is good customer recognition", says Alisdair Faulkner <u>@ThreatMetrix</u> <u>#ISMGFraudSummit</u> <u>pic.twitter.com/oPxm3OBxv5</u>

Mathew J Schwartz (@euroinfosec) <u>September 23, 2014</u>

95% of everything is good customer recognition, isn't it? And this is why the combination of secure hardware, local biometric and authentication and transaction-specific credentials (hello Apple Pay) can deliver both the security and the privacy through a simple and convenient tap that the new retail environment demands. Apple are not visionaries and nor am I. Dr. Who had it right from the start.

Chapter 5: Payment Systems

Payments systems are integral to transactions, obviously, and right now they are subject to intense pressures, both from the legacy infrastructure and existing businesses and from the new technology and new entrants. There is so much going on it is hard to know where to focus, but I hope this selection of blog posts will help.

Why are efficient payments subsidising inefficient ones? (3rd March)

Suppose someone wants to carry on using a product or service that suits their needs but imposes a general level of harm on everyone else? I might decide that I want to use depleted uranium for my dustbin and it's hard luck if it causes metal poisoning in my neighbours. Or I might decide that I want to use leaded petrol. Or cash. Should I be allowed to carry on regardless? I used this argument today in a discussion about carrots and sticks around payments, and it reminded me of something I read last year.

A prepaid card means she has to change completely her behavior — and while it makes the government more efficient, it makes my mom less so. That simple thing, which seems perfectly logical, creates a problem rather than solving one for her. At 78, she just says thanks, but no thanks.

[From Commentary - Emerging Payments Goes To Washington | PYMNTS.com][60]

How do you stop people from using the wrong kind of payments? You'd think that price would be the obvious mechanism, but I do have to say that this is not always true. The nice people from the Government Banking Service (GBS) very kindly invited me along to give a talk at a seminar they organised at Her Majesty's Treasury a while back. The seminar audience was made up from central and local government, and I may not have been sensitive to all of the nuance of their questions, since I'm not terribly familiar with the sector, but the essence of the day was that the British government is about to begin the re-procurement of banking services and since they currently handle about £900 billion in payments per per annum, that's quite a big deal. (The current contract is split between RBS and Citi, by the way.) One of the examples given to illustrate the scope for improvement in the sector was that of a government department that had instructed 150 CHAPS transfers last year. Analysis

---

[60] *http://pymnts.com/commentary/emerging-payments-goes-to-washington?utm_source=December+3%2C+2012&utm_campaign=Dec+3+NL&utm_medium=email#.ULyt-55iPnU.twitter*

showed that 125 of these were for less than £10,000 (the average CHAPS transfer is £2m) and could have gone via FPS at a tiny fraction of the costs. But they didn't. The people in the departments, just like the above commentator's mom, want to carry on doing what they've always done and since they don't see the price, why shouldn't they?

You could frame this issue in another way: to what extent should taxpayers subsidise people who want to use expensive alternatives? There was an interesting comment early in the day from a GBS speaker who said that he didn't want the public sector to end up as the last users of cheques and have to bear the whole cost of the infrastructure. Indeed. But shouldn't this be true for cash as well? Shouldn't the last people who want to carry on using it be paying for it?

This isn't a UK problem, it's a general problem. I noticed this comment from Olivier Denecker at the management consultancy McKinsey. He says that

> Even though Europe has a fairly advanced banking infrastructure, its payments products boast inherent cross-subsidies between products.
>
> [From #Economics of #Payments: how to remain #profitable][61]

Indeed. And the cross-subsidy is from the more efficient payment products to the least efficient ones, which cannot make sense in the longer term. It is time for action, although I'm not really sure what that action might be, other than to pass a law requiring all merchants to include the cost of "debit" transactions in advertised prices and allow them to recover the cost surcharge for all other choices.

Friction in the US payment system (10th April)

In his keynote at the Early Warning Summit 2014, David Pogue said that conference slogan should have included "reducing the friction in payments". That's a great slogan. So where is the "friction" in the US payment system? As far as many people are concerned (apart from the retailers who have massive lawsuits against the card schemes, naturally) it's all tickety-boo. Sucharita Mulpuru, a Forrester Research VP, is of this mind:

61

http://www.transactives.com/onpayments/epcasummit/News/tabid/814/YearMonth/201210/ItemID/71/Title/EconomicsofPaymentshowtoremainprofitable/Default.aspx

We don't fundamentally have friction in payments in the U.S. People who want to use cash are using cash for a reason: They prefer to or they don't want to be traced. As for credit cards, there is not something fundamentally inconvenient about them. They're fast, they're reliable, our networks are good

[From Quote About Why E-Wallets Have All Been A Total Disaster - Business Insider][62]

I think this represents rather a narrow perspective. Yes, OK, there are drug dealers and corrupt politicians and tax evaders using cash, but as for the rest of us there's nothing fundamentally inconvenient about cards? That depends on how you measure the costs and benefits, doesn't it?

Because our payment system is broken and does not have real security in place because the credit card companies that control the system can push the costs of fraud onto retailers.

[From Broken Payment System Guarantees Another Breach Like Target - Bank Think Article - American Banker][63]

This may be a harsh phrasing, but it makes a valid point. Just as an engine loses energy because of friction, so the economy loses energy because of payments friction. Effort that should be spent on developing new products instead goes on papering over the cracks; effort that should be spent on helping customers gets diverted into annoying them and effort that should be going into creating fantastic new services instead goes into PCI-DSS certifications and sending out breach letters.

And so one way to think about credit card fraud, is credit card fraud is a two-to-three percent drag on the entire economy.

[From Freakonomics » Why Everybody Who Doesn't Hate Bitcoin Loves It: Full Transcript][64]

I enjoy payment card fraud as much as the next man, but this is something of an exaggeration. I'm pretty sure the cost of the US payment system as a whole isn't two or three percent of the entire economy. Credit card fraud as measured by the issuers is around seven basis points. That's still a few

---

[62] *http://www.businessinsider.com/quote-about-why-e-wallets-have-all-been-a-total-disaster-2013-12*
[63] *http://www.americanbanker.com/bankthink/broken-payment-system-guarantees-another-breach-like-target-1064784-1.html*
[64] *http://freakonomics.com/2014/03/27/why-everybody-who-doesnt-hate-bitcoin-loves-it-full-transcript/*

billion dollars, but it's a tiny fraction of the volume of charges running through the system.

That's not the end of the story. To these fraud losses have to be added the cost of trying to prevent the losses due to the hello-1949 infrastructure. When you add in the costs of CNP fraud born by merchants, fraud written off as bad debt, the cost of PCI-DSS and everything else, it's still less than one percent. But it's still way too much and the root cause is, as Marc Andreessen points out in his piece, the system was never designed for use in the modern economy.

> The US leads the world in card fraud, at least in part because it has lagged in the adoption of the EMV (Europay, MasterCard and Visa) Chip & PIN standard, and continues to use signatures for verification. One result, said Carolyn Balfany, group head for US product delivery at MasterCard Worldwide... is that the US leads in card fraud with 47% of local fraudulent transactions although it does only 23% of the transactions globally.
>
> [From Lack of EMV means US leads the world in card fraud » Banking Technology][65]

I do remember, as an aside, that the question that was nagging me throughout the Money 2020 session last year on EMV migration in the USA was about the roadmap. If the payments industry, regulators and other stakeholders had some sort of roadmap for the evolution of retail payments (they don't) so that EMV was a step rather than the goal, then what is :

a) the goal, and

b) the plan B to take the industry forwards to that goal in case the US decides to ignore EMV and move on to the next big thing?

We've got a few ideas in both cases. The status quo is unsustainable.

In payments, the US is an emerging market (18th April)

The Bill and Melinda Gates Foundation is most, and deservedly, well-known for their work in tackling big, big problems such as eradicating polio. But what you may not know is that they have a programme called Financial Services for the Poor (FSP) which aims to help people out of poverty by providing digital financial services (DFS). The Foundation

---

[65] http://www.bankingtech.com/173772/lack-of-emv-means-us-leads-the-world-in-card-fraud/

decided to create an external advisory group to help to steer, support and promote DFS. This is called the Platform Enablers Group, because the Foundation sees DFS as a platform for products and services that will make a real and sustained difference to the lives of least well-off around the world.

I was flattered to be asked to be part of this advisory group and honoured to be able accept (on behalf of my colleagues at Consult Hyperion who actually do the ground-breaking work in delivering financial services in Kenya, Nigeria and elsewhere). There are two reasons for this:

The altruistic reason: my colleagues at Consult Hyperion have done some amazing work, from the original feasibility study for M-PESA to the implementation of TAP, and it feels good to be able share some of the experience and expertise to help the Foundation change lives.

The selfish reason: the other members of the advisory group are really smart and really interesting and I learn a tremendous amount from listening to them (especially when they argue - there's no quicker way of learning about a subject than hearing two people who know all about it disagree!).

At a recent meeting of the group, there was a discussion about trying to identify the key conditions for payment innovation that could help with financial inclusion and therefore with social inclusion. The group discussions are according to the Chatham House rule, so I can't attribute these comments (other than to say that they come from a very clever and very experienced person and I always take her opinions very seriously) but I wanted to share the three enablers discussed.

A reliable and efficient **identity infrastructure**. I will blog about this again some time in the future as I have been exploring some ideas about emergent identity infrastructures for emerging markets and I think there may be breakthrough strategies here. In many countries there are no ID cards, no population register and no consistent identifiers, so the cost of bringing customers into a system while complying with demanding KYC/ATF/AML (CDD) requirements is a barrier to progress. What if we made it easer for people to join the system and then defined their identity as the reputation generated within the system that could be later bound to external identifiers?

A **real-time settlement system**. Being able to move money instantly from one account to another works fine when both accounts are in the same system (such as M-PESA). But to scale, we need to be able send money between accounts with different organisations and even different kinds of institutions (e.g., between a bank account and a mobile operator account).

There are a few different ways that this can work, as my colleague Dick Clark explained at the Mobile World Congress this year.

> *As part of this work, MMU released a new paper titled 'A2A Interoperability' last week at Mobile World Congress in Barcelona that we co-authored with Consult Hyperion.* [From New publication: A2A interoperability – making mobile money schemes interoperable | Mobile for Development]

If it were possible to move money between payment accounts instantly (as you can do via the Faster Payment System, for example, in the UK) then it would mean that risk associated with a rich, multi-organisation environment would be reduced significantly.

A **regulatory environment** that allows new competitors to challenge the incumbents. The US has no equivalent of the EU's Payment Institution (PI) licence, but this would be a practical way to allow new entrants access to the infrastructure needed to deliver great new products and services.

I couldn't help but remark that the US has none of these with the result that, as another of the advisors pointed out, there are something in the region of a hundred million people in the US today who are unserved or underserved by the existing financial services providers.

> *For consumers, the costs of using cash are regressive and fall heaviest on the "unbanked" – mostly low-income individuals who can least afford it.*
>
> *[From Cash Is a Wasteful System, but Hard to Replace - Room for Debate - NYTimes.com]*

There are people trapped in the cash economy all over the developing world, and therefore denied access to the first rung of the ladder out of poverty, but there are people trapped in the cash economy in the developed world too.

The US and Japan are special cases for mobile payments (2nd June)

An interesting discussion about the relationship between age and payment mechanisms in a meeting this week reminded me to look again at Japan to see how the combination of money, technology and an ageing population come together to shape retail payment trends.

> *The number of prepaid electronic money cards in circulation hit 182.17 million in June, or triple what it was five years ago, a*

recent Bank of Japan survey said... growing at an annual pace of 15 percent to 20 percent in recent years... The BOJ credited the surge to people in their 30s who were the first to use the technology when it debuted and have since shed their privacy concerns to adopt it.

[From Use of prepaid e-money cards soars | Japan Times]

Edy is by far the most commonly-used e-money service, predominantly on cards although an increasing number of consumers are using it on their phones as well. It remains a fact though — as Dean Bubley observed in a Twitter conversation on such — that most consumers with contactless phones still use their cards rather than the phones. That's not to say that the use of contactless phones isn't growing for other purposes. I guess it just means that payments are not as much fun as rice cooking...

Appliance makers in Japan are jumping on the smartphone bandwagon with new appliances that can communicate with smartphones. Panasonic will launch a steam microwave oven and two induction heating rice cookers on 1 June that can communicate with Android-based smartphones. The appliances also use the FeliCa contactless technology.

[From Japan sees rise in smartphone-connected appliances - Telecompaper]

Another little window into the future is the use of NFC to provide a convenient and simple interface between healthcare devices, a crucial segment of the internet of everyone else's things in an environment evolving to support the elderly.

...healthcare equipment maker Omron has launched the Wellness Link service which allows users with Android and FeliCa-equipped handsets to track their health online with data obtained from the equipment, which includes scales, thermometers and blood pressure gauges...

[From Japan sees rise in smartphone-connected appliances - Telecompaper][66]

All very interesting. But back to payments. I thought that the most interesting quote in that Japan Times article came at the end.

---

[66] *http://www.telecompaper.com/news/japan-sees-rise-in-smartphone-connected-appliances*

Yasuhide Yajima, chief economist of NLI Research Institute, said the use of e-money cards will continue to spread because elderly people feel safe using them and they can be handled like cash.

[From Use of prepaid e-money cards soars | Japan Times][67]

In the UK, we seem to think that the elderly must be supported using cash and cheques because they are incapable of adapting to modern technologies. I suppose that's just one of the ways that Japanese payments are evolving differently from ours. Another is the central role of the mobile operators in driving interoperability and new services.

Japan's leading mobile operator and provider of integrated services centered on mobility, and KT Corporation, South Korea's leading telecom operator, have agreed to develop a cross-border e-money service that would enable DOCOMO customers with compatible smartphones purchased in Japan to use a prepaid e-money service called "Cashbee" in South Korea... Cashbee is available at some 52,000 locations in LOTTE Group department stores, convenience stores and mass transportation facilities such as subways and buses. The service currently has 5 million users.

[From New DoCoMo Fact Book - NFC Deal with KT | Wireless Watch Japan][68]

DoCoMo are also building interoperability in other directions, to make it easy for Japanese consumers to use their phones to pay elsewhere. Telcos in the Europe and the US have not gone down this route because they have adopted the EMV standard that provides interoperability for them, but the DoCoMo route does show how you could use NFC terminals to run non-EMV payment systems.

The collaboration will connect DOCOMO's domestic payment network to the world, enabling customers using iD mobile credit payments with compatible DOCOMO smartphones to make contactless payments outside of Japan, anywhere MasterCard® PayPass™ is accepted.

[From MasterCard Connects NTT DOCOMO's Domestic Payment Network to the World | MasterCard Social Media Newsroom][69]

---

[67] *http://www.japantimes.co.jp/text/nb20121127a6.html*

[68] http://wirelesswatch.jp/2012/10/10/new-docomo-fact-book-nfc-deal-with-kt/

The Tomorrow's Transactions Reader 2015

Now, no-one should imagine that US or European markets are going to evolve mobile contactless like, say, Japanese or Korean markets have done. These are markets with entirely different structures and entirely different market dynamics. As Consult Hyperion has long advised clients, we should look to these markets for inspiration and ideas but not for templates.

So, I think it's a mistake for anyone really in the U.S. or developed countries to be looking at Japan as a model for mobile payments.

[From The Future of Mobile Payments][70]

David Evans is right about this. But I'd go even further. Not only is Japan not a model for the US, the US isn't a model for anywhere else either. **Both** the US and Japan are special cases. I am not saying this in hindsight: it has been part of the Consult Hyperion mobile world view from the earliest days. That's why the trick in Europe is to look and learn from those markets but not to try and copy them.

Family faster payments (27th June)

Nick Reynolds posted an observation about interpersonal payments within family units.

"Dad, can you lend me a fiver?"

In a world with cash:

"Yes of course just let me dig through my loose change, there's always some hanging about in the drawer"

In a world without cash:

"Oh, err, I'll have to switch the broadband on... hang on a minute the wifi's down, err... what about my phone... err, the Bluetooth isn't working again I can't sync our accounts together... err... where's that contactless payment card,... err... it won't let me transfer anything we must be over our limit... err... sorry..."

---

[69] http://newsroom.mastercard.com/press-releases/mastercard-connects-ntt-docomos-domestic-payment-network-to-the-world/
[70]

http://www.frbatlanta.org/podcasts/transcripts/paymentsspotlight/111116_evans.cfm?d=1&series=Podcasts

---

[From "Dad, can you lend me a fiver?" in a world without cash | Nick Reynolds At Work]

Of course, Nick could always write out a cheque and have his son scan it with his phone which, given the comments in the Treasury's recently released paper on "Speeding Up Cheques", appears to be central to the government's vision of a new and better Britain. I have to say I'm not the least bit interested in this mode of working. I have a cheque from British Airways in my bag right now: when I got it, I didn't think "Oh goody, I can scan this with my Barclays mobile banking application — which, actually, I can't — and thereby have it clear in three days instead of four". I thought "why oh why didn't they just send the money either to my bank account via the new-fangled Faster Payments Service (FPS) that we hear so much about these days". They could have PingIt or Paym'd the money to me. They could have refunded it to the British Airways American Express card that I've used with them for a decade or so. But a cheque?

Anyway, back to Nick's scenario. This isn't how it works in our house because we are a modern family with mobile phones. And there is never cash in the drawer, ever. Therefore the exchange is rather different:

PingIt request "can you lend me a fiver?"

Confirm.

Er, that's it..

[From "Dad, can you lend me a fiver?" in a world without cash | Nick Reynolds At Work]

In a world in which there is an immediate settlement system so that you can transfer money between banks in (effectively) real time, there is no need for cash even with the family unit. And there is no requirement for geographic coincidence so the desperate pleas for train fare home late at night can be actioned without getting out of bed. Come on Nick. Get with the programme, Grandad, this isn't the US or France..

Contactless control (6th August)

In the UK there are around 38m contactless cards in circulation and their use is growing around 20% per month as I write. Clearly, customers like them. I'm sure many people share my attitude of mild annoyance at having to insert a card and enter a PIN instead of just tapping and going. And I do wonder about the risk analysis around using a card with a £10,000 credit limit and entering a PIN that might get shoulder surfed by a caffeinated ne'erdowell who is going to pick my pocket in order to buy a £2 coffee.

The Tomorrow's Transactions Reader 2015

There are, however, some security perceptions around contactless that we (technologists) should not ignore. In fact, if we address them, then contactless can be an even better proposition all round. I was thinking this because I wrote a piece about contactless crime and I've been thinking about it some more in connection with one of Consult Hyperion's projects for a major card issuer.

> During sentencing this week of a woman who had used someone else's PayPass debit card more than 30 times before being caught, the magistrate, Michael Wheeler, of the Perth Magistrates Court, said they were all too easy to use unlawfully.
>
> [From Tap-and-go fraud: MasterCard downplays consumer concerns | World | The Guardian][71]

In the UK customers are not liable for unauthorised contactless transactions and the issuers have a variety of techniques (and EMV risk management parameters) to play with to control risks. So the money isn't the issue. The damage here is to the image of contactless cards, not the issuers' balance sheets or customers' pockets. Consumer worries about security (no matter how ill-founded) are increased because of stories like these.

> Consumers remain wary of new "contactless" payment technology – with one in four saying they find the idea of paying without entering a pin number "scary".
>
> [From Consumers unimpressed by 'contactless' payments - The Scotsman][72]

Those you who listened to my podcast with Karen Williams from SpectrumInsight will remember that "crime" was one of the keywords associated with contactless and survey after survey (none of which I can be bothered to Google right now) has shown that consumers have genuine fears about security in the contactless payment environment. After all, we've spent the best part of a decade trying to persuade them to enter PINs!

One possibility for making customer feel more confident is to give them more control. I've often wondered why my bank doesn't give customers more control over transactions in general, not only contactless ones. Through my online banking portal I should be able to ask the bank to, for

---

[71] http://www.theguardian.com/world/2014/jul/11/tap-and-go-mastercard-downplays-consumer-concerns
[72] http://www.scotsman.com/business/finance/consumers-unimpressed-by-contactless-payments-1-2912134

example, automatically decline all magnetic stripe or non-3DS transactions on my debit card. Similarly, a customer who doesn't like contactless should be able to tell the bank to automatically decline contactless transactions on their card (this wouldn't stop a thief from using a card offline, at least until it is reported stolen). People might even decide to log in when they get home and turn off their contactless cards completely until they go to work the next morning, or that sort of thing.

Now, I know what experts in risk analysis for payments systems (e.g., the people I sit next to down at CHYP End) will say about this. They will point out that the loss to issuers is negligible so it's not worth investing in. But I wonder if the existence of such an on-off switch might be beneficial in other ways?

I have some evidence for this from the long ago days of Mondex. The cards could be locked using a four-digit pass code, something that customers had requested in focus group discussions. But the only way to lock the cards was using the hardware electronic wallets and the phones that few customers had. Therefore all of the shops that accepted Mondex had to be fitted with a lock/unlock device. As it turned out, customers never bothered locking their cards and never used the lock or unlock stations, but it was the fact that the lock existed and that the lock/unlock stations were visible that gave them confidence in the system. Maybe we could learn something about confidence from this and apply it to contactless? It doesn't seem that complicated to add a line of code to get the issuer hosts to auto-reject contactless transactions if the "no contactless" flag is set.

I think this is worth an experiment. If customers could choose through their online banking portal or mobile banking app to turn on or off contactless acceptance for their cards then they would use the cards more even though they never actually bothered to turn off contactless acceptance. After all, payment is one of those areas where confidence, perception and impressions of security are as important as the underlying reality.

Incidentally, when I asked our risk management wallahs about all this, they accurately pointed out that this is yet another argument in favour of using smart devices (e.g., mobile phones) for payments rather than cards because then all of the decisions will be (literally) in the hands of the consumer. Don't like contactless? Turn off NFC on the phone. Like contactless for credit but not for debit? Then don't put debit cards in your Google / Apple / Facebook (* delete where applicable) wallet. If your phone, rather than your card, gets stolen you tend to notice and can remotely wipe it. However you do the calculations, phones are more secure than cards..

The Tomorrow's Transactions Reader 2015

The value in payments isn't payments (15th August)

My old friend Peter Vander Auwera posed a good question on Twitter recently: "In 20 years, will merchants be willing to pay twice: once for the payment transaction and once for the relationship?"

Well I think I know the answer to this one. Not because I have any sort of crystal ball but because I can see the same trends that everyone else can see. The transaction revenue from payments (at least in the mass-market retail space) is asymptotic to zero. Payments are becoming a commodity and they'll soon be vanishing inside the transaction itself. At every conference I go to nowadays, people point towards the retailer apps as the transaction wrapper and I am sure they are right to be looking in this direction, although there will, of course, be others.

(As an aside, this has rather an interesting set of implications for incumbent players since I cannot even remember whether I've loaded a Visa card or MasterCard into my apps let alone which issuer the cards came from. I just don't care, and I'm pretty sure a great many other consumers won't care either, especially when the app provider offers them double loyalty points to go straight to the bank account.)

The incisive point in Peter's comment is that it will be the relationship that is the source of the value around the transaction and that will be what the stakeholders will pay for. Obviously, in order to have a relationship the counterparties have to know (let's set aside what that means for a moment) who each other is. They have to be able to **recognise** each other. And over time the **relationship**, and the history of the transactions associated with that relationship, become a most valuable asset indeed: a **reputation**. This is what we have taken to calling the "3Rs" strategy for businesses who want to exploit the triple-A technology play of authentication, apps and APIs that we have been advising them on for a couple of years.

> *That means that the future value – literally and figuratively – will accrue to the platform and the apps and the third parties that operate, power and enable the layers around payment that get consumers to buy more things.*
>
> *[From 2013 - The Unexpected Power Shift In Payments | PYMNTS.com][73]*

Well, not more things, necessarily, because the retailer's goal might be to get you to buy more expensive things instead, but Karen was certainly correct, provided that the payments layer can be made to work properly.

---

[73] *http://www.pymnts.com/briefing-room/consumer-engagement/Loyalty/2013/The-Unexpected-Power-Shift-In-Payments/*

That also implies a payments layer that is less vertically integrated, because it cannot predict or constrain the apps that will use it, and it should consume standard services from below (authentication being a good example).

One answer to Peter's question, then, is that the merchants won't pay twice, because the payment will be free. A potential commercial structure is that the merchant will pay for the recognition, they will manage the relationship themselves and they will sell the reputation on. Sounds plausible.

Chapter 6: Cash and Cash Replacement

This is pretty much the sharp end of the electronic transaction revolution, the "last mile" for the technology revolution and the dematerialisation of transactions. When it comes down to it, can we get rid of cash?

Crime correlates cash (4th April)

I got into an interesting discussion about bank robbery at a recent lunch. We were talking about risk and risk analysis. It happens that Consult Hyperion has a very well-developed risk analysis methodology (it's called "Structured Risk Analysis", or SRA) that has been used rather successfully on a wide variety of transactional services around the globe to help clients to evolve security architectures and to direct countermeasure expenditures effectively. I was trying to make some points about why proper risk analysis like this is a more cost-effective way to proceed than (for example) panicking about newspaper stories on hacking, and that led to a train of thought around cost-benefit analysis for the robber, not the bank. Are robbers put off by thick doors and barred windows and such like? Are robbers deterred by visible, physical symbols of security?

The security of physical buildings is no longer as important for financial services.

[From CYBER SECURITY WITHIN FINANCIAL SYSTEMS NEEDS TO BE FRONT-OF-MIND][74]

This is a fair point. So it set me thinking: if you are an amoral sociopath desperate for money, are you better off robbing a bank or working for it? As a responsible father, I want to help my teenage sons chart the best course for life. Right now, they are intent on going to University to study socially useful subjects in science and engineering, whereas I am trying to persuade them to become Somali pirates or Wolves of Wall Street. Having studied science and become a wage-slave trapped in mortgage serfdom I understand that side of the equation, but am less certain of the other. So I started off by reading a paper called the *Decision-Making Practices of Armed Robbers* by Morrison and O'Donnell.

This paper is based on a study of commercial armed robbery in London, UK, involving the analysis of over 1,000 police reports and inter- views with 88 incarcerated armed robbers.

---

[74] *http://www.globalbankingandfinance.com/cyber-security-within-financial-systems-needs-to-be-front-of-mind/*

The paper, being about UK robberies, contains an interesting snippet: a great many of the armed robbers in the UK use imitation firearms even though they have ready access to real ones. I imagine that in the US the use of imitations is vastly less prevalent, since it's presumably harder to buy an imitation gun than a real one there. But I digress.

> *almost all of these robbers evaluated the offence as having been financially worthwhile (aside from the fact that they were eventually caught and punished for their crime).*

So robbing a bank seems like good idea, if you exclude the possibility (in fact, the likelihood) of being caught. I suppose this is standard "Wolf of Wall Street" thinking though isn't it?

> *Neither does it seem practical to expect financial institutions and commercial properties to reduce counter cash much more than they already have.*

I disagree, of course. This is exactly what we should expect them do, since as far as I am aware there is a direct and measurable relationship between the amount of cash (more on this later) and the amount of crime.

> *Even when the amount of money obtained was quite small (an element often touted in support of the irrationality of economic criminals), it must be recognised that even apparently small sums may be adequate for the offender's immediate needs. Hence, gains may be subjectively much larger than they appear*

So even though the rewards of armed robbery seem to me, an educated middle-class professional, to be rather low, they are still sufficient to attract the robbers, because their needs are immediate and limited. The guy in the Nixon mask isn't robbing a bank to pay his way through college or to obtain seed finance for a brilliant start up idea, he just needs to buy a car or some drugs or whatever. This article seems, then, to indicate that so long as there is some cash in the till, there will be robberies. This is not an observation confined to banking.

> *Our results indicate that the EBT program had a negative and significant effect on the overall crime rate as well as burglary, assault, and larceny.*

> *[From Less Cash, Less Crime: Evidence from the Electronic Benefit Transfer Program][75]*

---

[75] *http://www.nber.org/papers/w19996*

What they are talking about here is the use of Electronic Benefit Transfer (EBT) programmes in the US, whereby benefit recipients are paid electronically and given cards that they can use in shops instead of being given cash. The authors found a 10% drop in crime correlated with the switch to EBT. It seems pretty overwhelming evidence, and even more so if you read the paper, which notes no impact on crimes that do not involve the acquisition of cash. If we can stop armed robberies, that would surely be an excellent social benefit to the move to cashlessness and would help us to explain the nature of appropriate regulation to legislators.

But back to the specific point about the relationship between bank cash and robberies. What should we do about it, other than the obvious, necessary and socially-beneficial step of abolishing $50 and $100 bills (as well as £50 note and €100, €200 and the €500 "Bin Ladens" as well)? It looks as if the answer is, essentially, nothing.

But with most robbers taking a mere pittance and bank robberies being a relatively rare crime (there are more than 6,000 commercial banks in the United States and thousands more credit unions), it's barely worth it for banks to invest in the screens, which cost a couple thousand per teller window to install... Overall, it's probably not worth it to attempt a bank robbery, the researchers conclude. "The return on an average bank robber is, frankly, rubbish," they write. "It's so low that it is not worth the banks' while to spend as little as [$7,000] per cashier position at every branch on rising screens to deter them."

[From What You Should Know Before Robbing a Bank - US News and World Report*]* [76]

The armed robbers, like everyone else, follow the money - literally - and so cash-in-transit (CIT) robberies are now the preferred option. We see the same in Europe where countries that have much higher usage of ATMs have much higher CIT robbery rates than countries that have lower ATM usage (see, for example, Sweden and Denmark).

In 2004, there were more than 7,500 bank robberies in America, 26 percent more than there were in 2010. According to the researchers, "robbing banks is no longer what you could call the crime of choice." But they do have some other advice: "Security vans offer more attractive pickings."

[From What You Should Know Before Robbing a Bank - US News and World Report*]*

---

[76] *http://www.usnews.com/news/articles/2012/06/11/what-you-should-know-before-robbing-a-bank*

Overall, then, we see another early indication of the emerging post-cash era: Spending on physical bank security is being reduced and spending on virtual bank security is being increased. We do, indeed, live in interesting times..

Business owners and cash (7th May)

Well, the gauntlet was well and truly thrown down on Twitter. There was a Twitter exchange (I don't really want to label these enjoyable interludes "discussions", but I can't think of a better word) on the back on Jim Marous' post on the use of cash in the USA, triggered by the Federal Reserve study on same. I wrote a guest post for Jim to build on his comments about this study, but in the course of the Twitter exchange I happened to see this from an interested member of the general public.

> *@dgwbirch @JimMarous cash is king cause taxes...Cause anonymous. You academics are a riot. write a blog post...Or talk to any business owner*
>
> *Ben_Katz (@Ben_Katz) May 6, 2014*

I can do better than that "ben_katz" -- I can point to several business owners who say that they would prefer electronic payments to cash. (Yes, I'll admit, these are the honest ones, but I don't think it should be core social policy to reduce transaction costs for criminals.) Last week, the *Jeremy Vine Show* on BBC Radio 2 had an interesting phone-in segment on cash. They had a taxi driver complaining about cash and lauding contactless and mobile solutions, a sandwich shop owner talking about the problems of managing cash float (and change) and someone complaining about parking machines. They were all challenging the assumption that the inertia around cash means an insurmountable barrier to change. It does not. The honest retailers also want it to vanish in favour of more efficient electronic alternatives.

> *I'm a retail manager. Please, please, please, for the love of god, let cash die already. It's expensive to store, sort, count, and transport. It goes missing. It falls apart. It sticks together. It slows down the checkout process.*
>
> *[From Paper Or Plastic: How Americans Buy Stuff, In 1 Graph : Planet Money : NPR][77]*

---

[77] *http://www.npr.org/blogs/money/2014/01/14/262502269/paper-or-plastic-how-americans-buy-stuff-in-1-graph?sc=pmapp&f=93559255*

This plea by itself would merit comment here, but what particularly fascinated me was the manager's subsequent comment about power and fallback, which we have discussed here before. In that particular shop, I imagine that the POS terminals are handheld devices with rechargeable batteries.

And losing power and/or communications does NOT stop us from accepting cards. It will, however, prevent our CASH registers from operating in a secure and audit able fashion.

[From Paper Or Plastic: How Americans Buy Stuff, In 1 Graph : Planet Money : NPR][78]

And if the POS terminals run out of juice after a few hours, then the store manager could just use a Square or an iZettle and get on with things. Note, however, the manager's emphasis on the final point: auditable. Getting rid of notes and coins and replacing them with electronic payments has implications for retailers beyond the cost savings of cash handling and paying taxes in a fair market is one of them that we all accept.

Cash hits the excluded (23rd May)

As Professor Douglas McWilliams entertainingly described in his Gresham College lecture *Prostitutes and software developers -- A short history of the Italian black economy* (14th February 2014*),* Italy decided to revise its GDP calculations back in 1987 in order to obtain membership of what is now the G8 by including estimates for its "black economy" in the figures. When these estimates were added, Italy's GDP surpassed the UK's and Italy was asked to make a greater contribution to the European Union! Oops. Anyway, to restore fair contributions, some years later, European Union statisticians revised their methodologies to treat the black economy equally in all EU countries and things like software and drug-dealing and prostitution were added to the figures in 1995[79].

In Diane Coyle's excellent "GDP: A Brief but affectionate history", she talks about this statistical revision and says that "the largely cash-based informal economy of moonlighting, avoiding taxes and regulations, but creating work and output, has been placed inside the production boundary". So it's measured, but the people in that economy are not contributing their fair share to the national piggy bank. We [the payments

---

[78] *http://www.npr.org/blogs/money/2014/01/14/262502269/paper-or-plastic-how-americans-buy-stuff-in-1-graph?sc=pmapp&f=93559255*
[79] *The UK's decision to revise GDP statistics in this way led to the European Commission's demand for an additional two billion euros contribution in October 2014*

industry] don't spend much time thinking about the black economy, but it's an untapped market for electronic payments. Why? Well, yes, there's a tax penalty to switching to electronic payments, but on the other hand dealing in cash is not always the optimum transactional solution. There are problems living in a cash economy.

> *When I went to a strip club where I could pay in Bitcoin, a dancer told me she had been tipped in Japanese and Pakistani currency in the past and had no idea what it was worth until she went to a money exchanger to cash it in. The latter wasn't even worth changing for dollars.*
>
> *[From 21 Things I Learned About Bitcoin Living On It A Second Time][80]*

I was fascinated by this story about the weakness of cash in relation to Bitcoin and it reminded me of something I'd seen elsewhere about the relationship between cash and, and I hope readers of a gentle disposition won't be offended by this phrase, "sex workers". People who live on the margin get screwed by cash.

> *In the eastern Indian city of Calcutta, a non-governmental organisation has started a programme to help sex workers recognise fake currency given to them by clients,*
>
> *[From BBC News - Teaching Indian sex workers to spot fake currency][81]*

I can genuinely say in all of the impassioned rants against cash that I have made at industry gatherings, it had never occurred to me that one of its failings was that people would use counterfeits to defraud prostitutes. So another count is added to the prosecution charge sheet. It transpires that prostitution is illegal in India (where there are some three million prostitutes) so sex workers cannot complain to police if they are paid with fake notes.

> *But a campaign group known as the Committee for Indomitable Women has now begun a training programme in Kolkata's notorious Sonagachi red light zone, where an estimated 8,000 sex workers ply their trade.*
>
> *[From Indian sex workers learn to spot counterfeit currency - InterAksyon.com][82]*

---

[80] *http://www.forbes.com/sites/kashmirhill/2014/05/15/21-things-i-learned-about-bitcoin-living-on-it-a-second-time/*
[81] *http://www.bbc.co.uk/news/world-asia-india-21940666*

Should I ever go to Calcutta, I swear I will go to meet the Committee for Indomitable Women and offer them my full support and a mobile POS. In a country where counterfeits are widespread, it is obviously the marginalised groups trapped in the cash economy who are the big losers. Fortunately, the Indian central bank has decided to help out a bit by withdrawing some of the most counterfeited notes (those printed before 2005, which the RBI says are printed in large quantities by "neighbouring countries".

What's my point? Well, we need to provide payment systems that deliver privacy (not anonymity) so that we can provide better alternatives to cash for people who live in the margins. They deserve better than cash..

Scandinavian models and Russian cash (5th June)

In the UK we love a good episode of The Killing or The Bridge. I'm a big fan. (Wallander not so much.) One thing I kept thinking when watching The Bridge recently was how the mobile phone had been integrated into the crime drama. The mobile phone changed crime drama for good. Now you have to have complicated plot devices around why someone doesn't have a phone, or a signal, or has two phones, or can't be tracked or whatever. Then it occurred to me that when the Scandinavians get rid of cash, they will have to rewrite the crime drama again.

Get rid of cash? Yes. Look at how things are developing over there. In Sweden for example. In the old days, there were domestic debit cards in Sweden: BankKort and Sparbankskort. These were free to customers, who mainly used them to get cash from ATMs. Credit card volumes were low. By comparison with their Nordic neighbours, the Swedes were heavy users of cash (and hence saw far more armed robberies than their neighbours.

In 1995, the Swedes decided to ditch the domestic debit cards and replace them with scheme cards. So Visa Sweden and EuroPay Sweden sprang up -- with a system of bilateral interchange fees (there are now 29 issuers and 10 acquirers who have these agreements, which are not seen -- as I understand it -- by Visa or MasterCard) -- and began to market cards as an alternative to cash. And they had success. Today, there are no paper cheques and debit card transactions dominate at point of sale.

If you look at Swedbank as an example, they have seen debit card transactions go from 12m in 1995 to one billion today while ATM transactions have grown only from 50m to 85m. A pretty successful effort

---

[82] *http://www.interaksyon.com/article/72255/indian-sex-workers-learn-to-spot-counterfeit-currency*

by any measure. More than 97% of Swedes have debit cards (these are issued to citizens from the age of seven years up, with parental permission) and more than 99% of merchants accept cards, with the consequence that 80%+ of retail transactions are card (it's about half in the UK and about two-thirds in the US).

The Swedish Central Bank's goal has begun to be achieved, in that Sweden is one of the few countries in the world where the cash "in circulation" is actually falling. However, as the Riksbanken said back in 2012, the use of cash even in Sweden is still far too high compared to where it should be on the basis of social costs (because debit cards have the lowest total social costs. They want to drive cash usage down still further.

Niklas Arvidsson at the KTH Royal Institute of Technology in Sweden predicts that paper money and coins will disappear from Swedish society - "but probably not before 2030," he says.

[From The cashless society is closer than you think | ScienceNordic][83]

Cards will not, of course, be the final nail in the coffin for Swedish cash. That honour will go to the mobile phone. But there is still work to be done. Niklas goes on to say "It would also have to meet several requirements, such as good emergency backups. People would need to be able to pay even during power cuts, or when electronic systems crashed or were hacked. Currently cash payment is the only system that never fails, so it's difficult to see how we could go totally cashless."

As I've mentioned before on the blog, the reason why I am curious about the Swedish situation is that in Sweden the anti-cash alliance is a broad church, embracing not only banks and law enforcement but the trade unions and the retailers.

Swedbank is piloting the use of mobile couponing with merchants in Uppsala, the country's fourth-largest city which is bidding to eradicate cash as part of a local crime-fighting initiative.

[From Finextra: Swedbank pilots mobile couponing in cashless utopia Uppsala][84]

Not everyone is heading down this same path, though. While most of the bank branches in Sweden are now cashless, there are still reactionary forces at large.

---

[83] *http://sciencenordic.com/cashless-society-closer-you-think*
[84] *http://www.finextra.com/News/FullStory.aspx?newsitemid=24395*

In fact, for three of the four major Swedish banks combined, 530 of their 780 office no longer accept or pay out cash. In the case of the Nordea Bank, 200 of its 300 branches are now cashless, and three-quarters of Swedbank's branches no longer handle cash... Fewer then 10 of Handelsbanken's 461 branches currently do not handle cash and the bank's goal is to have cash in every branch by the first quarter of 2013.

[From Sweden's War on Cash Runs Into a Wall–and a Heroic Bank :: The Circle Bastiat]

Hurrah for competition. So long as the three major bank's electronic payments are not cross-subsidising Handelsbanken's cash then no problem. When I say that the anti-cash movement is broadly-based, by the way, I really mean it. And they have a great figurehead too: Bjorn from ABBA. I loved the interview with him in the "Digital Values" magazine, where he comments that Sweden, Denmark and Norway would be the ideal countries to go cashless first (of course, I'm hoping Scotland will beat them to it after hearing my talk to the FS Club in Edinburgh back in April). But listen to him: he is spot on!

Go Bjorn! "It is completely incomprehensible why Sweden's central bank is to issue a new series of notes from 2015"

Go Bjorn! "Who needs 500 Kroner or 1000 Kroner notes?" (and as far I as understand the situation, the Swedish banks have said essentially the same thing to the central bank).

Go Bjorn! "The problem of begging isn't a problem of payments or payments technology"

What a guy. He's even made the ABBA museum cashless! And when asked about that, he said "some people asked did we want to frighten away the Russians with their bundles of notes", which might well be a more general comment about activities in a number of European capitals. Incidentally, in the same magazine, Professor Kai Olsen notes that, of course, going cashless wouldn't eliminate crime but goes on to say that if the Nordics went cashless they would at least export some of their Eastern European criminals ("Digital Values", p.44). Which brings me to a serious point, that I raised following a super presentation by Kurt Gjesten from the Pan-Nordic Card Association at the PayComm MEETS 2014 event. Why aren't the general public more outraged about the use of cash to support -- indeed, subsidise -- a variety of nefarious activities?

Like many other Greeks, Mr. Mantzouranis said, Mr. Kantas would bring bundles of cash to his banker, who would fly to

Switzerland to make the deposits when enough cash had accumulated to make the trip worthwhile.

[From So Many Bribes, a Greek Official Can't Recall Them All - NYTimes.com]

I spoke to Kurt later in the day and we concluded that we (ie, the payments industry) need to become considerably more effective at communicating these issues to the general public. We can't blame them for remaining ignorant about the pernicious and revolting impact of cash on our civilised society if don't make an effort to explain them. I intend to start right away.

Cashless the Kiwi way (24th July)

Having had the opportunity to spend a few days in New Zealand and having been involved in a few different conversations with different organisations down there I thought it might be of mild interest to report back on how they are getting on on the road to cashlessness. I'll spoil the ending by telling you that they're doing pretty well.

I intended to conduct my usual experiment of turning up without any cash and just using cards but actually that's quite a boring experiment in New Zealand because virtually no-one uses cash and the overwhelming majority of retail transactions are on cards. When I first arrived at the hotel in Auckland and unpacked my suitcase, I realised that I'd forgotten to pack my deodorant so I strolled out of the hotel to see if there was a nearby pharmacy or convenience store. I wandered into the first one I saw and picked up a stick deodorant. I walked over to the clerk and…

I'll get back to that in a moment. The other experiment I was conducting on that trip was to play around with the new Travelex multi-currency cash card. I'd seen it advertised at the airport a couple of times and it struck me as being mildly interesting and since one of the currencies that it advertised was the New Zealand dollar I thought I'd give it a try. So I got one at Heathrow on the way out and loaded some NZ dollars on the card with the intention of comparing the exchange rates for loading dollars directly to the card with the exchange rate for using my UK credit card in New Zealand. Remember, I do this so you don't have to.

As another aside, which has no real bearing on the narrative, when I got to Sydney I noticed that Qantas were advertising a similar product in their lounge which was combined with their frequent flyer card and had quite a wide range of currencies. This struck me as rather a fun idea. If British Airways combined the Travelex card or something similar with their British Airways Executive Club card (I always have in my travel wallet anyway) then, hopefully, I could have got one without having to go through all of the relevant junk "know" your customer stuff at the airport.

I say that because I did find getting the card a bit of a pain. I went over to the Travelex desk and assumed that I would hand over 50 quid and be given a card that had 50 quids worth of NZ dollars loaded onto it but because of the stringent Know Your Customer, Anti-Terrorist, Anti-Money-Laundering and other pointless and dreary regulations I had to fill out a form then wait while they painstakingly typed the stuff from the form into a website and then typed in some more stuff about the card they were going to give me and so on and so forth. It wasn't quick or easy to get a prepaid card loaded with a couple of hundred NZ dollars. I had to fill in an application, hand over my passport (which was then photocopied) and provide mother's maiden name (I always give an invented one, for security purposes). I suppose it took 10-15 minutes. All of this despite the fact I wanted about a hundred quids worth of foreign currency and have been a customer of Barclays Bank for 37 years. Surely my debit card and PIN should have sufficed?

Stifling innovation will be the major consequence of this action, Shanahan said. "This will slow down the creation of new programs. Ironically, it's good for the people who are already in." The higher the bar set by regulators, Shanahan said, the more the advantage swings to players with established compliance programs.

[From Will The Bancorp Consent Order Hurt the Prepaid Industry? | Bank Innovation][85]

I do wonder if a normal member of the public would really bother with all of this but anyway, I did, so I had the card. At which point I remembered that they told me on Twitter that it doesn't come with an app, so to check the balance you have to log in on the web. But the point is, I had one, so when I went out of the hotel I went to an ATM to change the PIN on the Travelex card (which as it turned out, I couldn't do) and draw out some cash just to see that worked. Which it did, perfectly. That is how I came to have some NZ dollars in my pocket when I went to the convenience store. And so we can return to the story.

...proffered a $20 bill alongside the deodorant. The clerk to my surprise and delight told me that they **did not accept cash after 7pm** and that it was cards only. So I bought a large chocolate bar as well to reward the store for their forward thinking policy. Thus, there was not a single shop, restaurant, taxi or fast-food joint I visited that needed cash.

---

[85] *http://www.bankinnovation.net/2014/06/will-the-bancorp-consent-order-hurt-the-prepaid-industry/*

I saw plenty of contactless terminals and even a couple of vending machines that accepted mobile payments, contactless cards and (bizarrely) coins. I wanted to give QuickTap a try because it looked quite interesting but when I tried to download the app, nothing happened. Maybe you have to be logged in to the NZ iTunes Store or something ridiculous like that.

New Zealand is an advanced country that illustrates one of my all-time favourite quotes, from William Gibson's brilliant "Count Zero" Grafton (London: 1987): *It wasn't actually illegal to have [cash], it was just that nobody ever did anything legitimate with it.* The future may well be unevenly distributed, but some of it is in New Zealand.

(Oh, and as for the exchange rates, the NZ$ I loaded to my Travelex multi-currency cash passport were at 1.77 to the good old Pound Sterling, whereas when I used I my Amazon MasterCard to pay for dinner in Auckland the effective rate was 1.88 including the currency conversion charge.)

The British Cash Gap (21ˢᵗ October)

There is a growing "cash gap" in developed economies as the amount of cash in circulation races ahead of economic growth and in a superb new paper[86], the economists Jonathan Ashworth and Charles Goodhart delve into the fact that this is also true for the UK, noting that the ratio of currency to GDP in the UK has been rising, despite the greater use of card and online payments.

In their detailed examination of the statistics, the authors make a clear distinction between the "black economy" (e.g., drug dealing and money laundering) and the "grey economy" of activities that are legal but unreported in order to evade taxation. When your builder offers you a discount for cash and you pay him, you are participating in the grey economy. When your builder offers you crystal meth and you pay him, you are participating in the black economy. They define a total "shadow economy" as the sum of the black and grey economies. This shadow economy is growing and is costing billions (which mortgage-paying, PAYE-slaves like me have to make up for with our taxes).

> *Patrick Stevens, tax policy director of the Chartered Institute of Taxation, said: "These figures suggest that tax evasion and other illegal activity are costing the Exchequer nearly five times as much as tax avoidance".*

> *[From UK tax gap climbs to £34bn - FT.com]*

---

[86] *http://www.voxeu.org/article/trying-glimpse-grey-economy*

Hence the question as to whether the amount of cash in circulation might be in some way related to the shadow economy and me being taxed up the rear-end to provide services to self-employed tradespersons whose income comes in just under the income tax threshold? Are there other explanations? The authors note that there was a jump in the amount of cash in circulation around the time of the global financial crisis (which might be expected as the public saw television pictures of customer queuing to withdraw their money from Northern Rock) but that it did not fall back after stabilisation. Thus, they ask, is the amount of cash still high because the general public are concerned about the safety of banks (hint: no) or are there correlating indicators of a growth in the grey economy (hint: yes, ranging from the growth in self-employment to VAT increases and, hence my earlier example, housing repairs).

Charles and Jonathan refer to an older paper[87] "Is Cash Becoming Technologically Outmoded? Or Does it Remain Necessary to Facilitate "Bad Behaviour"? An Empirical Investigation into the Determinants of Cash Holdings" (London School of Economics: 2000) that looks in detail at the substitution of cash at retail point of sale (POS) and shows that ATMs and POS terminals have an impact on the demand for small notes but overall, and I think this is a really interesting and important point to bear in mind, the central conclusion is (as they say) "on our evidence, the effects of modern payment technologies on the demand for cash are not that strong".

Wow. That's huge. In essence, it means that the demand for cash from central banks is not to support the economy but to support crime. We need to have some joined-up thinking and it is time we tackle the issue of cash and criminality head-on.

Lots of shady activity may also be bad for growth. Shadowy firms find it hard to borrow, which limits their productivity. According to Francesco Pappada of the Einaudi Institute of Economics and Finance many small firms in Greece deliberately avoid taking out loans because it involves being more transparent. Unproductive firms pay low wages.

[From Greece's shadow economy: The treasures of darkness | The Economist][88]

But back to the point. Charles and Jonathan's work (which estimates that the UK economy is significantly bigger than shown in official figures) seems to me to explain the growing tax gap in the UK as well as some

---

[87] *http://www.lse.ac.uk/fmg/workingPapers/discussionPapers/fmg_pdfs/dp358.pdf*
[88] *http://www.economist.com/news/finance-and-economics/21623742-getting-greeks-pay-more-tax-not-just-hard-risky-treasures*

other strange economic behaviour around the labour market. Now, in a talk about electronic money that he gave a couple of months ago, Charles was kind enough to refer to some of my thinking around "privacy money" as a way forward so I'm going to promote some ideas around that to our clients in the payments world to see if there is a win-win around the corner..

Time to scrap metal (24ᵗʰ December)

There's a thing that economists call "the big problem of small change". If you're interested, there's a very good book about this, which is called "The Big Problem of Small Change". In essence, there's a problem because it's hard to make a living out of producing small change, so no-one does it. Therefore the State has to do it, and deliver "token" money that is supported by law. But as inflation erodes the value of the small change, it becomes increasingly unprofitable to provide it and the State has to bear the cost in the interests of the economy as a whole. This why you get apparently bizarre behaviour such as the US Mint producing nickels that cost eight cents and that people throw in the trash rather than carry around with them. If this was your business you'd get out of it.

Is it still in the interests of the economy as a whole to produce these stupid small coins? I have no idea why the Royal Mint are messing about wasting our money on making 1p and 2p coins that nobody uses any more. It's about time we recognised low-value coins for what they are.

"They are just scrap metal."

[From BBC News - Should the UK ditch the one penny coin like Canada?][89]

Now, if you want proof that our coins actually are scrap metal then instead of taking my intemperate ranting at face value you should, as the man says, follow the money. And in this case it leads to China.

Denmark has freed two Chinese held for 48 days after they tried to exchange a massive hoard of scrap Danish coins that were mistaken for counterfeit money

[From Denmark frees Chinese duo held in 'fake' coin mix-up | GlobalPost][90]

---

[89] *http://www.bbc.co.uk/news/business-21292441*
[90] *http://www.globalpost.com/dispatch/news/afp/131016/denmark-frees-chinese-duo-held-fake-coin-mix*

I thought it was a pretty unusual incident and I mentally filed it away to use as a conference anecdote at some point in the future. Then I spotted another similar case, and this caused me to suspect an interesting underlying story.

> *Two Chinese tourists have been briefly held in France on suspicion of forgery after trying to settle their hotel bill with one-euro coins. Police were called in after a hotel owner in Paris became suspicious about the two men, and 3,700 one-euro coins were then found in their room.*
>
> *But the coins were not counterfeit.*
>
> *The men said they had got the money from scrapyard dealers in China, who often find forgotten euros in cars sent from Europe.*
>
> *[From BBC News - Chinese tourists detained in Paris over one-euro coins][91]*

This tallies with the Danish story. European coins are being collected in Chinese scrapyards. Who knew! I feel sorry for these enterprising people because my relentless campaign to end the cash menace will one day result in their unemployment. But, for the time being, sufficiently large amounts of coins from Europe end up as scrap that it makes for a worthwhile enterprise (in China) to collect up these coins and ship them back here to use! How fun.

> *Italian police discovered over 500,000 euros' ($623,000) worth of counterfeit coinage from a Chinese mint on Dec. 12 in a container ship docked in Naples.*
>
> *[From Italian Police Arrest 4 Chinese in Biggest Counterfeit Case Since Introduction of Euro][92]*

Uh oh. If container-loads of euros are coming back to Europe from China, then it's inevitable that this trade will attract counterfeiters looking to make a rather slow buck out of the business. So what should we do? I have a cunning plan.

I suggest we make a virtue out of necessity. Since the Chinese gang responsible can presumably produce these coins at a lower cost than collecting them as scrap metal (otherwise they wouldn't make them, they'd just collect them), why don't we just stop producing coins above

---

[91] *http://www.bbc.co.uk/news/world-europe-24524699*
[92] *http://www.theepochtimes.com/n3/1144572-italian-police-arrest-4-chinese-in-biggest-counterfeit-case-since-introduction-of-euro/*

face value and sending them for scrap and instead let the Chinese counterfeits circulate in their place? Think about it. It costs the US Mint 1.66 cents to make a penny that no-one cares is real or not. So why bother? If Chinese criminals can produce one for half a cent, ship it to the US in a container and make a profit of 0.2 cents on it, let them.

Greece, Scotland and Ecuador (24th December)

The topic of currency popped up again this week because I happened to see a tweet from one of my favourite AFC Wimbledon fans, the Sky economics editor, Ed Conway. He was commenting on some of the ongoing troubles in Greece.

> *In 2012 Greece was far closer to leaving the euro than commonly thought. Do such concerns return to haunt the currency in coming months?*
>
> *— Ed Conway (@EdConwaySky) December 29, 2014*

A couple of years ago, when the Greek Euro exit was being discussed in another context, I made the point that I thought that, given new technology, the readjustment of currency zones might not be as difficult or a costly as some people were imagining.

> *Greece could pull out of the Euro and create a "hard e-drachma". There is no need for physical currency. It's badge of national vanity, just like an airline (and soon, an army) used to be. It would be no big deal to, over time, open e-drachma bank accounts, obtain e-drachma payment cards and so forth.*
>
> *[From What's a Grecian e-urn?][93]*

I made the same point, in a boringly consistent fashion, a few months ago when discussing the options for money and payments in a newly independent Scotland. As you might suspect, this idea is too good to be mine, and you are right. It is a mash up of some of the incredible work that my colleagues have been doing in the world of digital money and the vision of an under-rated Chancellor of the Exchequer.

> *John Major proposed an extremely sensible alternative to the euro, which at the time was labelled the hard ECU (and ignored)... The idea of the hard ECU was to have an electronic currency that would never exist in physical form but still be legal*

---

[93] *http://tomorrowstransactions.com/2011/09/whats-a-grecian-e-urn/*

tender (put to one side what that actually means) in all EU member states.

[From _What's a Grecian e-urn?_]

You can see why this idea is so appealing. It allows for progress in monetary reform at low cost and acts to remove physical cash from circulation where it causes nothing but mischief and costs. I had a fun conversation about this a few weeks ago when I wrote that "it looks as if the Royal Canadian Mint's Mintchip and Safaricom's M-PESA have been sitting in a tree, because the Central Bank in Ecuador is trying to launch a national mobile payment scheme that is designed to handle B2B transactions (along with P2P, top-up, cash in and out, in-store purchases and electronic receipts), deliver a very low rate (a $50 charge costs four cents, a roughly 0.0008 rate)". I remarked (in a private forum) that setting aside the feasibility, merits or purpose of such a scheme, you can't help but wonder why more central banks don't do this.

Now today I read that the Ecuadorian system is going live and the details have been made public. In essence a hard electronic currency is being created by the Central Bank.

Anyone over 18 can, nationwide, open your electronic money account for free, without the need to approach any window, typing the * 153 # on your cell phone with any mobile operator. Since then, users can open their accounts.

From mid-February 2015, the second phase will begin transactions loading, unloading, delivery of electronic money, people, receipts commercial, consulting and bank transfers.

Finally, the third phase will begin in the second half of 2015 with the incorporation of electronic money payment of utilities, tax obligations, orders and other use cases. Thanks to the model of electronic money the Central Bank of Ecuador, most transactions are free and the rest will cost a few cents.

[From _Google Translate_]

As I said, a cross between MINT and M-PESA, a centralised government solution to the big problem of small change that I wrote about again last week. An interesting aspect of this otherwise vanilla Unstructured Supplementary Services Data (USSD) pre-paid value transfer system is that will be denominated in US Dollars. The US Dollar has been legal tender in Ecuador since 2000, when the post-gold standard "Sucre" was abandoned (although, apparently, the "centavo" coins are still in use. What for I can't imagine, since according to my calculations there are two-and-a-half million of them to the US Dollar) so the unit of account will not be changing.

So why is this such a good idea? Well, you have to understand that the US Federal Reserve banknotes that are in circulation in Ecuador, stuffed under mattresses in Ecuador and fuelling the less-formal sections of the Ecuadorian economy are in essence an interest-free loan to Uncle Sam. By replacing these with an electronic currency, or I suppose more strictly speaking an electronic currency board, the Ecuadorian central bank can reclaim the seigniorage for itself. All well and good and the ability to transact electronically must also be of the great benefit to the citizens.

If the central bank were to ask the advice of people experienced in the creation of a national non-bank mobile payment system (e.g., Consult Hyperion) I am sure that they would be advised to make the system a platform for innovation to encourage entrepreneurs to build local solutions on top of it. If I might be as bold as to make a warning from history, though, I should add that such a system would also benefit greatly from transparent auditing as the citizens will not hold the electronic currency unless they are sure that it will remain redeemable at par for US dollars themselves. If the government were to fall prey to the temptation to put more of the electronic US dollars in circulation than they have (or have the equivalent of) in reserve then, as the Wall Street Journal[94] observed back in August, they will simply be creating doomed electronic assignats that will never obtain traction in the wider economy and Ecuador will be unable to reap the many benefits of its transition away from cash. After all, you cannot simply create US Dollars out of thin air by changing a few numbers in a computer somewhere.

P.S. In case you see any tweets, newspaper comment or learned articles that refer to this as a "cryptocurrency" please bear in mind that it isn't.

---

[94] *http://www.wsj.com/articles/mary-ogrady-ecuadors-phony-bitcoin-ploy-1408919820*

Chapter 7: Cryptocurrency

In the last couple of years, the topic of cryptocurrency has re-emerged in the electronic transaction world. The idea of money that can be created and traded without a central trusted body is fascinating, and we are a long way from understanding the implications.

Bitcoin exchange failures don't mean anything (5th March)

The media fascination with Bitcoin continues. The Sunday Times magazine led with a "who is Satoshi" this weekend (they don't know) and the BBC's Business Editor, Robert Peston, said last week that

> *What excites is the development, by Bitcoin enthusiasts, known as miners, of a super-efficient money transmission network on the internet,*

> *[From BBC News - Bitcoin's life-or-death moment][95]*

I would put it slightly differently: it's a digital asset transmission network, and electronic cash is only one of the kinds of digital asset that might be transferred and quite probably not the most interesting one (if you can transfer digital assets efficiently then you have no need to use cash as an intermediary). But some people are using it for cash, and having handed over that cash to people they had never met before and had no reason to trust, they are predictably upset that it has vanished.

> *Citing an unnamed company lawyer who also spoke at the press conference, The Wall Street Journal reported that MtGox had lost 750,000 bitcoins (around $412.5 million) belonging to customers, and over 100,000 bitcoins (around $55 million) of its own money.*

> *[From Having lost $468 million in bitcoins, MtGox files for bankruptcy protection | Ars Technica]*

On Twitter, I couldn't help remarking on the coincidence of the amount, which rather neatly matches the amount that seems to have gone missing from Citi at the same time.

> *as much as $400m was misappropriated throughout the course of the fraud*

---

[95] *http://www.bbc.co.uk/news/business-26335547*

[From BBC News - Citigroup profit hit by Mexican fraud][96]

Imagine trying to get $400m out of Citi by robbing branches with a shotgun! It is inconceivable. As the old saying goes, if you want to rob a bank, work for it. Which, in the absence of any verified facts whatsoever, leads observers to the natural speculation that Mt. Gox's money may have walked out of the back door rather than the front.

But I digress. Oh wait, another Bitcoin exchange has just been robbed and shut down. The question I am being asked repeatedly is what the Bitcoin exchange shenanigans mean for the long run. As I said when interviewed for the BBC Today programme, I strongly suspect that it means nothing. And the reason I say this is because as I have long and boringly maintained (starting back in 2011), I don't think XBT makes sense as a currency and I think the activity around the currency is a speculative bubble (as does Nobel Laureate economist Robert Shiller). I do drink the cryptocurrency kool-aid, but I see the advent of cryptocurrencies that embed values that make sense to wider communities. XBT is different. It isn't about values, it is about belief.

> *Bitcoin can't survive without manufacturing consent for its ideology.*

[From The Bitcoin personality cult lives on | FT Alphaville][97]

That may be true of the currency, but I don't think it is true of the technology, a genuine breakthrough. Right. I promise not post anything about Bitcoin for at least a week..

Bitcoin was not designed for retail payments (27th May)

Bitcoin doesn't make sense as retail payment mechanism and I cannot see why anyone would use it in a shop. There, I've said it. The comments will be predictable (and I will, of course, in the tradition of free speech and open debate publish the ones that I like) but I stand by that position. When I say that sort of thing in a public forum, I am immediately confronted with the example of Overstock.com and the vast numbers of merchants accepting Bitcoin and the number of startups looking to make accepting Bitcoin even easier. But I have a suspicion that merchants accepting Bitoin is more about marketing than sales.

---

[96] *http://arstechnica.com/business/2014/02/having-lost-463-million-in-bitcoins-mtgox-files-for-bankruptcy-protection*
[97] *http://ftalphaville.ft.com/2014/02/27/1783842/the-bitcoin-personality-cult-lives-on/*

One of the reasons this is worth mentioning is because at the beginning of 2014 there was an estimated 20,000 – 30,000 merchants that accepted bitcoins for payment. By the end of the first quarter, approximately 60,000 merchants accepted bitcoins. Yet there has been very little corresponding on-chain growth.

[From What Block Chain Analysis Tells Us About Bitcoin][98]

You see the point of this analysis. If you actually look what Bitcoins are being used for, it isn't buying stuff. In Erin McCune's excellent and highly-recommended write-up of Bitcoin 2014 in Amsterdam, she says that Bitpay is processing $1m per day for 30,000 merchants, which is about $30 per day per merchant, so maybe next quarter's blockchain analysis will show an increase, but I can't help feeling that it doesn't really matter.

Accepting Bitcoin as a merchant is a great way to get publicity but may not result in any actual Bitcoin business... However, most Bitcoin-accepting merchants are instantly turning their Bitcoin into cash.

[From 21 Things I Learned About Bitcoin Living On It A Second Time][99]

This is exactly what David Evans said in his piece about Bitcoin that attracted such an angry response from the Bitcoin community. I've just read his response to this and I have to say that I think he is right to say that "It hardly does the Bitcoin enterprise any good to create the false impression that bitcoin is becoming widely accepted by merchants". As the article I quoted says, merchants that do accept Bitcoin are "instantly turning their Bitcoin into cash" and there's nothing wrong with that. Well, "instantly" might be a bit of an exaggeration, but you get the point.

I wasn't able to buy lunch at Buyer's Best Friend because it took the Bitcoin network 67 minutes to confirm my $26/.0832 BTC payment

[From 21 Things I Learned About Bitcoin Living On It A Second Time]

It's not clear to me that Bitcoin was ever intended to be a retail payment mechanism, so it's not surprising that it is less than optimal in such an environment. After all, credit cards were never designed to work on the

---

[98] *http://www.coindesk.com/what-block-chain-analysis-tells-bitcoin/*
[99] *http://www.forbes.com/sites/kashmirhill/2014/05/15/21-things-i-learned-about-bitcoin-living-on-it-a-second-time/*

Internet, which is why they are less than optimal there and people are investing considerable effort in developing digital wallets. My point is that we shouldn't be surprised that Bitcoin is clunky buying noodles in a fast-food restaurant because that's not what it is for.

> *Ramen Underground in Japantown has been accepting Bitcoin payments since early spring. They don't accept Bitcoin at the restaurant's busier downtown location, because there's already a line and doing so would only slow things down.*

> *[From San Francisco's QuickCoin – Bitcoin so simple, even Mom can use it | PandoDaily][100]*

If the technology had been called Distributed Digital Asset Transfer or something else that didn't involve the word "coin" I wonder if so many people would be trying to bring it to the point of sale? As far as I can see, if you talk to people who are serious about investing in Bitcoin, it because they see where the technology is taking us rather than because they want to speculate on Bitcoins or bring them to the Taco Bell counter.

> *It's not the digital currency, but the underlying platform that will cause an enormous market disruption. Bitcoin is more than just another currency, it's "an Internet" for registering and transferring property.*

> *[From Bitcoin: It's the platform, not the currency, stupid! - The Next Web][101]*

I quite agree, and I think we've been accurate in presenting essentially this assessment of Bitcoin to our clients from the first time it impinged on business consciousness. Erin is absolutely right to say that the world of payments will face dramatic changes because of Bitcoin, but it won't be because people are using Bitcoin to buy pizza..

Bitcoin as flux capacitor (30th July)

The nice people at Mendeley asked if I could pop in and give a talk about Bitcoin round about the same time as I was asked to contribute a chapter to a new book about cryptocurrencies. So I thought I'd put the two things together and use the talk as a treatment for the book chapter.

---

[100] http://pando.com/2014/05/26/san-franciscos-quickcoin-bitcoin-so-simple-even-mom-can-use-it/
[101] http://thenextweb.com/insider/2014/02/15/bitcoin-platform-currency/2/#!v7fmA

As the title of the talk suggests, David actually goes back to the past in order to understand the future of money, and what it holds in store for all of us as transactions technology advances.

[From "Back to the Future of Money" David Birch Talks@Mendeley | Mendeley Blog][102]

I'm genuinely interested in getting your feedback as I have to sit down and work on the chapter shortly. I'm going to call it "Back to the Future of Money — Bitcoin as Flux Capacitor". Here goes.

Benjamin Cohen from the University of California, Santa Barbara, wrote a good book about the future of money, called *The Future of Money*, in which he sets out some of key issues around the topic. One of them is whether there is tendency to one currency in the future (something along the lines of the galactic credit familiar to science fiction fans) because the minimisation of transaction costs is the dominant, driving factor, or whether an explosion of currencies is likely because new technology minimises transaction costs in other ways? Cohen concludes that "the power of scale economies notwithstanding, monetary geography is set to become more, not less, complex" and he compares the future landscape to the "heterogenous, multiform mosaic that existed prior to the era of territorial money".

There is an interesting connection between Cohen's conclusion in his *The Future of Money* and the work of social anthropologist Jack Weatherford wrote a good book about the history of money, called *The History of Money*, in which he looks at the sweep of monetary evolution. Weatherford also observes that the future of money looks more like it did in "the neolithic world economy before the invention of money than it looks like the market as we have known it in the past few hundred years."

To see two experts from diverse fields come to similar conclusions, that we need to look to the past not the present to see the future, especially since this is the same conclusion that I came to from staring through my techno-deterministic crystal ball, leads me to conclude that we are heading into an era of monetary experimentation, fragmentation and innovation. As a technologist, I suspect that there will be more different kinds of money, not just more currencies, than ever before. In the chapter I will look at what these kinds of money might be and how cryptocurrencies might evolve to actually remove money from some kinds of transactions. I predict that at the end of the transition to cryprocurrency, the marginal cost of introducing another kind of money will be approximately zero. So we

---

[102] *http://blog.mendeley.com/talks-at-mendeley/back-to-the-future-of-money-david-birch-talksmendeley/*

will be in the "let a thousand flowers bloom" mode and might reasonably expect a rush to evolutionary dead-ends followed by mass extinction.

If this comes to pass, and we find ourselves in the neo-neolithic economy with a wide variety of currencies, what will it look like? I will also speculate on this in the chapter, but one interpretation might be to see a world of communities (geographic in neolithic times, virtual in post-modern construction) in which money is little-used within communities, but a variety of both types of money and currencies are used between communities.

If this analysis is anything like correct then it tells us that Bitcoin is not the future of money. Instead we should think of Bitcoin as the flux capacitor of "Back to the Future" fame. It is the key piece of technology that allows us to begin assembling a future economy that in many of its dynamics takes us to a richer and more diverse version of the past rather than a simplified version of the present.

Bitcoin is the start of disruption (7th August)

Steve Mott and I ran a somewhat experimental session on Bitcoin at the excellent BAI Payments Connect event in Las Vegas earlier in the year. Modesty forbids me from relaying just how well this worked, so I shall restrict myself to just one twestimonial:

> #payconnect Steve Mott and @dgwbirch team up for best payments presentation of all time! Good work @BAI and planning crew.
>
> Jim Bruene (@netbanker) March 11, 2014

My part in this session was to explain to a general banking audience that however sceptical they might be about the Bitcoin currency (XBT), and I share that scepticism, the blockchain technology is a genuine technological breakthrough and the start of a new era in transaction technology.

> The Bitcoin protocol (crucially distinct from bitcoin, the currency it underlies) was built from the ground up to support far more complex transactions and relationships than simple value transfers.
>
> [From Bitcoin is not just digital currency. It's Napster for finance. - Term Sheet][103]

---

[103] http://finance.fortune.cnn.com/2014/01/21/bitcoin-platform/

The Tomorrow's Transactions Reader 2015

One of the most interesting pieces that I've read about the more complex transactions was from Eli Dourado, who pointed out that more generalised transactions can solve a variety of real-world problems in an innovative and efficient way. Here is one example:

> The simplest variant is a 2-of-3 transaction. Let's say that I want to buy goods online from an anonymous counterparty. I transfer money to an address jointly controlled by me, the counterparty, and a third-party arbitrator (maybe even Amex). If I get the goods, they are acceptable, and I am honest, I sign the money away to the seller. The seller also signs, and since 2 out of 3 of us have signed, he receives his money. If there is a problem with the goods or if I am dishonest, I sign the bitcoins back to myself and appeal to the arbitrator. The arbitrator, like a credit card company, will do an investigation, make a ruling, and either agree to transfer the funds back to me or to the merchant; again, 2 of 3 parties must agree to transfer the funds.

> [From Stop Saying Bitcoin Transactions Aren't Reversible | Eli Dourado] [104]

Now this example, like a great many other examples, is about payments. But take this way of thinking and look at the classes of problems that it solves. It seems to me that there is a widespread (and general) set of problems around the creation, management and transfer of digital assets that could be solved in this way. I got involved in a fascinating discussion around this at an entertaining discussion session during Auckland's Nethui meet up and it left me thinking that idea of smart contracts around digital assets is more of a window into the coming economy that using Bitcoin to buy laptops from Dell, because trading without clearing and settlement is massively less expensive than trading with them. But how would this work?

> Long-term sustainability can only be achieved by providing an incentive for users to contribute to the network — for altruistic to selfish reasons — so that there are always a sufficient amount of resources available at any given time.

> [From Tomorrow's Apps Will Come From Brilliant (And Risky) Bitcoin Code | Opinion | WIRED]

Correct. So in other words, who will pay to do the distributed proof of work that is necessary to maintain a blockchain? In the Bitcoin world, the reward for doing the proof of work is the Bitcoins themselves and these

---

[104] http://elidourado.com/blog/bitcoin-arbitration/

are used as a currency (although technically they aren't really). So what if we forgot about the whole idea of Bitcoins as money and instead think of them just as a way of keep score with respect to maintaining the blockchain? Then a rather obvious alternative to incentivise people is just to pay them and treat the Bitcoins as a mechanism for recording who has done the work. If the people doing the work are the same as the network of people who are using the results of the work, then it would be possible to simply net off the resources and settle up periodically.

This is what I mean. Let's imagine that there is a network of financial services organisations that want to create a blockchain to provide a more cost-effective platform for the trading of some assets. You can imagine some form of bonds being handled in this way. So each of the financial services organisations sets up the equivalent of a mining rig to do the work. Each of the financial services organisations pays a small amount per transaction. At the end of the month the participants net up and if one of the organisations has contributed more to the network in terms of mining than they drew in terms of transactions, then they get payment from the rest of the network and vice versa.

This is why feel justified in saying that Bitcoin is indeed the start of disruption in business processes irrespective of whether Bitcoin the currency ever obtains mainstream traction. It is because the blockchain technology, the open public ledger with distributed proof of work, is a genuinely new way of solving a problem in the digital world and solving it in a way that has no physical analogue at scale..

Bitcoin, currency and competition (8th October)

I'm thinking about currency and competition because, and I imagine I'll get trolled for saying this, I had good fun arguing with some of the Bitcoin folk at Innotribe this year. I learn quickly by arguing with smart people but it's fair to say that not everyone has the same educational policy.

> *Innotribe's bitcoin series included talks on regulation, disruption and the future of investment in the space. The crowd, comprised of a mix of digital currency veterans and novices alike, displayed an enthusiasm and critical eye that largely defined the day's events.*

> *[From Bankers Debate Bitcoin at Sibos 2014][105]*

That critical eye included me for one. I remain sceptical about Bitcoin as a currency while I remain enthusiastic about the potential for blockchain

---

[105] *http://www.coindesk.com/bankers-bitcoin-sibos-boston/*

technology (and, indeed, other kinds of blockhains and other kinds of virtual currency). By coincidence, the week before Innotribe, we had had our annual Unconference at Google in New York, where Jeffrey Robinson had given a talk about his new book.

Although Jeffrey Robinson, an author and journalist, described the digital currency as a fraud, he said the underlying technology was "brilliant."

From Payments Industry's Focus Turns to Fraud, Security at PaymentsSource[106] .

In fact, in Jeffrey's book *BitCon: The Naked Truth About Bitcoin* (Sep. 2014) he quotes the Nobel prize-winning economist Paul Krugman as saying that "there's a good case to be made that bitcoin is impressive technology for payments, but why a bitcoin itself should be something of value is not easily answered". Quite. Bitcoins are a means of keeping score in maintaining the distributed public ledger, but it seems to me to be something of a leap -- with a logic that eludes me -- to see that score as being a currency or to see the blockchain best used for retail payments.

Anyway, I enjoyed Jeffrey's book and found it an interesting perspective on a hot topic. Having spoken to Jeffrey at some length and interviewed him for a podcast, I think it is reasonable to say that one of his observations is that some Bitcoin devotees exhibit cult-like behaviour. I know this will result in a deluge of abuse via anti-social media, but I actually think he is right about this, and I'm not sure it helps to advance the cryptocurrency case. I keep seeing this kind of thing...

Rather than spending their time hiring lobbyists to try to convince governments to legislate against cryptocurrencies and the block chain

[From How Banks Can Cash In On Bitcoin - Informilo][107]

I don't believe this for a moment. Having been involved in a number of conversations with regulated financial institutions, and working as I do for a company that provides paid professional services to more than one of the same in connection with cryptocurrencies and the blockchain, I can tell you right now that I have **never** heard even one banker ever say any such thing. Never. Nor have I ever heard of any bank hiring lobbyists that are anything to do with Bitcoin at all one way or the other

---

[106]

[107] *http://www.informilo.com/2014/09/banks-can-cash-bitcoin/*

The disturbing truth for many in the Bitcoin community is that the majority of bankers really don't care. If Bitcoin becomes a digital asset with a liquid market then they will trade it just as they trade frozen orange juice futures (this is real, by the way, it wasn't made up for *Trading Places*). If Bitcoin becomes the only money in the entire world, I'll still need to borrow it from a bank to buy a house or car so they will lend it to me.

I was accused of being "vile" on Twitter for saying this sort of thing, an accusation I refute in every degree. Perhaps it was a little strong to refer to the "libertarian fantasies" of the Innotribe panel but I think I stand by the substance of the comments, and I do not restrict them to Innotribe. I was amazed to see similar comments from the head of the UK's Competition Commission.

> *Alex Chisholm, chief executive of the Competition and Markets Authority, said the success of bitcoin would depend on trust but had the potential to liberate people held down by corrupt governments.*

This seems to me to be an entirely unjustified utopianism that highlights precisely the strange cult around Bitcoin. This is exactly what people (e.g., me) thought about the internet a generation ago and I can't see much evidence that the hapless inhabitants of North Korea (to pick just one example) are any more free because of TCP/IP. It's the same utopianism that people had about communism between World War I and World War II, the same utopianism that people had about America in the 19th century. But I digress. Mr. Chisholm went on to say that

> *"It's very welcome to see competition in the market, like many others," he told the Institute of Directors' annual gathering at the Royal Albert Hall.*

Well, I for one would love to see the Competition and Markets Authority launch an investigation into why there is only one Bank of England, one Pound Sterling and one interest rate for the whole of the UK, so more power to his elbow. I wonder if this is the sort of thing the Government were hoping for when they pointed Mr. Chisholm? I do hope so.

Private money and privacy money (13th August)

A resurgence of interest by journalists means that I am once again drawn to Bitcoin and the question of whether Bitcoin or some other cash replacement technology is the future. I generally send the journalists to sleep with my standard four hour lecture on the history of the impact of technology drivers on the functions of money and end up by telling them that Bitcoin isn't like WoW Gold or PayPal. Bitcoin is a different beast: Bitcoins aren't like Amazon Coins or online game credits because they combine the mechanisms for exchange with the store of value. Bitcoin is therefore much more interesting, which I why I take an interest in the evolution of (and learning from) the Bitcoin ecosystem even though I remain sceptical of its long-term traction as a currency. And why I was so happy to see my old friend Jon Matonis on the agenda at the EPCA in Brussels last year. It's important to have serious debate on these issues with serious thinkers. (There was a definite connection between Jon's excellent presentation on Bitcoin at the EPCA and Bernado Batiz-Lazo's talk on the paleo-future of cashlessness at the Tomorrow's Transactions Forum in London, by the way, in that they both used the word utopian.)

Jon and I agree on a lot of things. For example, I'm not sure I buy Douglas French's bullish take on Bitcoin at the Laissez-Faire Club, but I think Jon and I share his take on private currency as part of a spectrum of future currency choices. The way that money works now, with fiat currencies under the control of nation states is a transient implementation. There is no reason to imagine or expect that it is the only, or optimum, way of organising money. It may well be that private currencies, for example, are the future.

Maybe what the banking industry is really afraid of is the Amexes and Wal-Marts of the world creating their own currencies and banking systems.

[From Currencies of the Future | Laissez-Faire Bookstore]

Indeed, I was pontificating on the same not only in my book chapter but also at the wonderful Cafe Scientifique at our favourite pub down at CHYP End, The Keystone, when they invited me along last autumn. I'm not sure that the banking industry is absolutely as frightened about this as the Bitcoin acolytes think: if Wal-Mart ran the world's money and Sam's Shillings were the official currency of the USA, I'd still need to borrow some from Wells Fargo if I wanted to buy a house.

So what don't Jon and I agree on? Well, Gizmodo had an article about the technologies that we will still be using a couple of decades from now. One of them was, as it happens, cash.

In the information age, paying by cash is the best way to keep your purchases anonymous. Aside from simply preserving your privacy, paper money is a great shield against identity theft, because the payee doesn't even get your name, let alone an account number. The government would probably love to end the use of cash, because it allows payees to keep illegal transactions off the books, but paper money is the only form of payment that doesn't require a third party like a bank to get involved.

[From 15 Current Technologies We'll Still Be Using in 2030]

It does require a third party (like the US government, in the case of Benjamins), but that's not what I want to argue about. It's that point about anonymity as a desirable characteristic of a cash replacement technology that I want to drill down into and explore.

As society goes increasingly cashless, payment companies will have a larger business, and a more valuable one, in closing the loop for offline transactions and helping deliver customers. The data they possess is without equal; did somebody buy something? How much did he spend? What did she buy? Paper money cannot be tracked in this manner.

[From Payment Data Is More Valuable Than Payment Fees | TechCrunch]

This last point is very, very crucial because it touches on the privacy issues that will be central to any realistic plan for realising the value of this data. These are perfectly reasonable concerns. But they are a plea for privacy, not anonymity.

Now, in some of the online discussions around Bitcoin, this anonymity is held to be most important in a political context, to stop the godamn federal government from taxing the sheeple. But it seems to me that If I disagree with government policy on, for example, taxation then I should either move to another jurisdiction or vote for change. Using cash and not paying my taxes (thereby increasing the tax burden on my fellow taxpayers) is not the right choice, moral, ethically or practically. The right answer is to get society to work out where it wants to set the privacy dial and then get the technologists to implement it. If we are given an unambiguous statement of requirements then we (the payments industry) are perfectly capable of designing a solution. Since no-one seems to know what these requirements are, some form of strongly-authenticated pseudonymous solution seems the right way forward to me.

Cash is not a metaphor for freedom, it is a requirement of freedom. A strong society that accepts human nature without moralizing will always have anonymous cash. Only totalitarian governments — where everything not expressly required is illegal — would want to monitor the flow of every cent.

The Tomorrow's Transactions Reader 2015

[From <u>Anonymous Cash = Freedom | Stowe Boyd</u>][108]

There are, it seems to me, two things wrong with this argument. First, cash is not a requirement for freedom. They have cash in North Korea and they don't have cash in Norway (well, they do, but only for criminals). Second, the tension isn't between total anonymity and total surveillance but between the faux anonymity of an industrial society and the managed pseudonymity of the post-industrial society. Let me explain what I mean by each of those points.

Freedom is a political term in the sense it is being used here. If you live in some countries, then you don't have any freedom and it doesn't matter whether you are using cash or a credit card. I don't think it helps the discussion one way or the other. Whether you think that Bitcoin is a Zionist plot or the last redoubt against the Zionists of the Federal Reserve (both opinions I've heard expressed in the Church of Bitcoin), it's got nothing to do with democracy.

Anonymity makes for a more interesting discussion. I don't want to live in a society that allows anonymity for all but the smallest transactions. I want to live in a society that provides the appropriate level of privacy. If all transactions are anonymous, then the rich and the powerful are not accountable. I'd rather all transactions were public than all transactions were hidden.

Which means we either continue to obscure and socialise financial information for the sake of retaining a truly fungible and anonymous bearer currency system — i.e. we allow the government to replace the private banking system's money creation function — or we opt for the sort of transparency and personal accountability that kills the anonymous function of cash entirely.

[From <u>Gorton's battle of light and dark money | FT Alphaville</u>][109]

This choice is false. The right solution is privacy-enhanced money (PEM or, as I think I will call it, X$), not anonymity. Money that remains private in the normal course of events but if there is a fraud or some other crime, or if the police have a warrant following due process, then the veil can be peeled back and the transaction details revealed. I think that when it comes to anonymous cash, the bad outweighs the good.

---

[108] *http://stoweboyd.com/post/2358837421/anonymous-cash-freedom*
[109] *http://ftalphaville.ft.com/2013/10/28/1679132/gortons-battle-of-light-and-dark-money/*

Bitcoin, in an odd way, is a step in the right direction. The blockchain tells me that Wallet X sent a Bitcoin to Wallet Y, but I don't know who wallet X and wallet Y belong to. One might imagine a future version of a blockchain where I don't know who wallet X and wallet Y belong to, but I know that (say) the "system" does and will reveal so under warrant. So, for example, if you want money from me and you send me a certificate that contains a Bitcoin public key that is digitally-signed by a regulated financial institution, then I can be confident I am actually sending money to my gardener and not an Eastern European fraudster, So who could sign the key? It would have to be someone who has carried out the relevant KYC on the key owner and can keep their personal data secure. Let's a call it a "bank", for the sake of argument..

Banks and blockchains and clouds (10th December)

The kind people at Barclays invited me along to their "Distributed Banking" workshop to explore some new possibilities around the blockchain, cryptocurrency, digital identity, cloud computing and such like. A lot of the workshop discussions were fun, but the highlight of the day was, for me, getting to argue with John Clippinger. I've followed John's work for years, and his 2007 book "A Crowd of One" greatly influenced the evolution of my thinking around digital identity. We agree on a great many things, including the key role of pseudonymity in workable, scalable digital identity proportions for the mass market but we found a few things to disagree on as well. I learned more about the future of identity debating with John at the workshop than I would have learned in a month of reading papers and magazine articles.

So what could a bank do in this space?

Well, a couple of years ago I saw a presentation on the IRMA project (IRMA = "I reveal my attributes), a research project underway at the Rabboud University Nijmegen. The goal of the project was to implement attribute-based credentials (along the lines of U-Prove or Idemix) but optimised for implementation in smart cards. Having the keys stored in tamper-resistant hardware simplifies, as I understand it, the cryptography needed to implement what they refer to as "self-blinded" credentials. The reason for doing this is, of course, to implement pseudonymous credentials that can be used in transactional environments which is why I was paying attention to the work.

Now that Apple have put their seal of approval on the use of tamper-resistant hardware, in the form of the Secure Element (SE) inside the iPhone6, I think it might be time to revisit this kind of attribute-based approach that depends on having cryptographic processing inside tamper-resistant hardware.

The Tomorrow's Transactions Reader 2015

To see what I mean, consider this practical example. The bank generates a key pair and loads the private key down into the SE of my mobile phone (there is, by the way, an alternative vision whereby it is the mobile operators that generates a key pair and loads the private key into the SIM). The bank puts the corresponding public key into a directory that anyone can now use to find the key and send secure, encrypted messages to me. The bank keeps the private key safe and sound so that if I drop my phone down a toilet they can reload the private key into my new phone.

Now, an obvious first use of this technology is for the bank itself since the bank will often want to send secure messages to an app on the phone. When the app receives such a message it sends it off to the SE to get the session key decrypted using the private key and then the app uses the session key to read the message. These are tried and tested cryptographic techniques and the implementations are well-known and well understood.

But we can go further. The bank can attest to any number of attributes on my behalf and then create public key certificates (certs) that it can either download to the phone or keep in its cloud and download pointers to the phone. A simple example might be a cert that says that I am over 18. So to use the traditional example in these cases, I go to create an account at an online gambling site and when I am asked to demonstrate that I'm old enough to play I send the cert (or, more likely, under hood and invisible to me, a pointer to the cert in the bank cloud) to the gambling site. The gambling site retrieves the certificate from the bank cloud and encrypts a challenge using the public key it found inside that certificate which it then sends to the bank app on my mobile phone (or of course it might send it to a gambling app on my mobile phone). Now the only way that that challenge can be answered is if it can be decrypted using the private key that is stored inside my SE so the app sends the challenge down to the SE at which point I am asked to authenticate myself to the app, using TouchID, let's say. I put my finger on the sensor to authenticate and then the challenge is decoded and answered. Now, the gambling site knows for certain that the person at the keyboard or tablet or smartphone has control of the private key (which we might, for sake of argument, call the digital identity) of a person known to the bank, even if they don't know who the person and even if the bank doesn't know that the gambling app has used the key.

Now, you wouldn't use a system like this to launch nuclear missiles. Here's are examples that show why. A parent in modern Britain might well lend their iPhone and fingerprint to their pre-teenage son or daughter in order to let them stick a few quid on Manchester City to get a draw at Roma tonight egged on by Ray "'ave a bang on that" Winstone. Agents of a foreign power might steal your phone and obtain your fingerprint from the case and use it make a pretend finger and... you get the point. It is not perfect security, but generally speaking authenticated control of the private key should be good enough to allow a retailer, bank, government department or other service provider to depend on the attributes provided in the certificate from the bank. Here's another example.

A reader wondering whether or not to make a purchase might be convinced by this breathless praise: the only problem is, Jelly Bean and Nicodemus Jones are both the pseudonyms of Ellory himself, who was outed this week by fellow crime writer Jeremy Duns as the author of 12 glowingly positive writeups of his own books on Amazon, as well as two reviews critical of his fellow crime authors Mark Billingham and Stuart MacBride.

[From Sock puppetry and fake reviews: publish and be damned | Books | The Guardian][110]

Now, as an author myself, I might be very tempted to log in on Amazon under a false name and give myself a rave review. I would never do this, of course, because I am a gentleman and could not live with the shame, but if I did, it might be nice for Amazon to ask for a cert that says that I am over 18 and live in the UK. Then, if it sees the same public key being used to complete reviews under other names, it can not-name but shame me and block my reviews. (Of course, if I'm dedicated, I might open 12 different bank accounts and get 12 different keys, but sooner or later I'd trip up and get found out - look what happened to the Dread Pirate Roberts.) I might even want my "review identity" to be out there on a blockchain with all of my reviews so that my "review reputation" can be independently verified across lots of different sites, not only Amazon. I want my reviews to be given more weight and to be taken more seriously, so I want my reputation to be public even if I don't want my real name to be public.

Keeping my real identity tidily locked away at the bank while I navigate my way around the new economy using attributes seems most appealing to me. The more you are required to give up your real identity on the web, the more likely it is to be compromised. I saw an example of this just the other day.

Police are investigating after internet hacking group Anonymous "compromised" the security of a web forum and obtained the private email addresses of officers.

[From News - Latest breaking UK news - Telegraph]

---

[110] *http://www.guardian.co.uk/books/2012/sep/04/sock-puppetry-publish-be-damned*

This an absolutely text book example of the case in point. First of all, I strongly doubt whether either the "web forum" or "Anonymous" have any idea whether any of the e-mail addresses belong to officers or not, since there's no way for the web forum to have people prove that they are police officers before joining and, secondly, unless the police officers involved had not the slightest notion of how the interweb tubes work, none of them would have used identifiable e-mail addresses.

If were to log on to a web forum for disgruntled Consult Hyperion employees to complain about the antics of their Global Ambassador then I would do it as theogenes.de.montford (at) hotmail.com, not dave.birch (at) chyp.com. You get my point: if I we had a working identity infrastructure then the web forum mentioned in the above example would be able to demand the IS_A_POLICE_OFFICER attribute and this attribute would be a linked to a conditionally-anonymous identity (i.e., a pseudonym).

This overall approach might be summarised as "real reputations not real names" and this is where the blockchain could be a breakthrough. If reputations are committed to the blockchain and cannot be changed (after all, once I'm over 18 I'll always be over 18 - no "right to be forgotten" applies here) then I can keep attributes in a wallet to use them as and when. My name, my address, my favourite hobby and my inside leg measurement could all be there (attested to by trusted sources) ready for me to use. Here I am convincing Marco Crispini from Matrix Vision that this is the right approach.

I see this shift to a reputation-based approach as being a crucial component of such a scalable identity management system and so (I think) does John. Your name and other personally identifiable information are, in this model, just more attributes and are not privileged in any way. If you want to tell the gambling site who you are, that's up to you, but they won't get it as a byproduct of age verification. It's easy to construct examples where this could be the major selling point of such a system. If I log onto an online dating service then potential mates might well expect to see attributes from third parties that they trust to attest to the fact that I am a real person, I am over 18 and I am resident in the UK. I might want to save my real name for the first date though.

Part 3: Markets
Chapter 8: Finance and Banking

Electronic transactions have been at the heart of the finance and banking sector since the first Western Union wire transfer in 1871. Whatever technologists might think about the sector, we need to understand its dynamics and response to new transaction technologies and the new business opportunities they provide.

Why is there a magnetic stripe on my card? (29th January 2013)

I think it is important to understand what the general public think about things, no matter how ignorant or uninformed their views are, so I often read the comment threads under newspaper articles with more interest than the articles themselves. Take, for example, a recent Guardian piece on chip and PIN in the US (not!). In the comment thread, someone asked in passing as to why their (French) payment card had a magnetic stripe on it. This made me think, because two of my UK payment cards have been recently cancelled and reissued (at a cost of £££ each time). In both cases they are UK issuers bearing the cost of US fraud. In both cases they have been reissued with a pointless stripe. Is this really sustainable?

One of the cards, that I sometimes use for business expenses, was replaced a couple of weeks ago. My issuer called and told me that the card had been counterfeited and used (of all things) in a car wash in North America. I doubt that international criminals were after high-limit cards to use in car washes, so I assume they'd used it in the car wash to see if it had been cancelled yet. I asked the nice woman on the phone if they could reissue the card without a magnetic stripe on the back and automatically decline further magnetic stripe transactions. She said (in essence) that that option wasn't in her script, so no.

Then I had a call from another issuer, saying that another of my cards was being cancelled and reissued because it had been reported compromised in a US data breach. I don't remember shopping at Target in the last year (although I may well have done) so it must be another retailer. I don't actually use that card much in the US so I suppose I could go back through statements, but hey, I've got client work to do today. The two other UK credit cards that I use from time to time (but don't take overseas) are so far safe. The only other UK card I take to the US is my debit card, and that also remains safe because of my heightened security.

"I would never use my debit card... in a shop or online – only in an ATM," Mr Birch says. "...mobile is far more secure than cards."

[From <u>Mobile apps boost payment security - FT.com</u>]

I did indeed tell the FT that I only ever use my debit card in ATMs. This is because my debit card, although it has a highly secure chip on it and that chip contains a highly secure EMV application, is undermined for transactional purposes. For unfathomable reasons my bank has chosen to glue a trivially-counterfeitable magnetic stripe to the back of my debit card, added embossing to it and even put my bank account and sort code details on the front. Bizarre. I don't want the stripe, and I want my bank to automatically decline all stripe transactions whether at POS or ATM. Nor do I want embossing, and I want my bank to automatically reject any "zip zap" transactions. Nor do I use the card online, so I want my bank to decline all CNP transactions except those made with UK merchants (personally, I don't really want to use it online at all but some merchants such as the DVLA surcharge credit cards by more than the useless Avios or minimal cashback on my other cards is worth). By and large, unless incentivised otherwise, I'd rather use credit cards because of the combination of rewards and protections that they bundle. I am genuinely mystified as to why people use debit cards, but they do. MCX will have to deal with this as well.

Without offering consumers something equivalent, MCX Retailers will find it exceedingly difficult to convince customers to switch.

[From <u>Lessons from a breach | Drop Labs</u>][111]

I can easily imagine that retailers will (successfully) bribe consumers to opt for ACH-based transactions with less consumer protections in return for loyalty points, coupons and the like. I wonder if the potential for reduced hassle because of increased security might also be factor?

This was brought home to me in ironic fashion because of the second call. They asked me to verify that certain transactions had, indeed, been made by me or my good lady wife. The transactions I was asked to verify included a chip and PIN transaction in a local petrol station. If I were a normal member of the public, and someone called to asked me to verify a chip and PIN transaction, then I would either conclude that something had gone horribly wrong with the chip and PIN system and that my chip had been cloned or that I was not talking to my issuer at all but sophisticated Eastern European fraudsters.

---

[111] *http://www.droplabs.co/?p=964*

The Tomorrow's Transactions Reader 2015

I'd already ruled out the latter possibility. When they first called me and asked me to confirm some personal details, I had naturally assumed them to be sophisticated Eastern European fraudsters, hung up and called back using the number on the back of my card. At this point, I was able to confirm all of the transactions. Anyway, they sent us the new cards. For me this wasn't terribly inconvenient because I have loads of cards so I just started using one of my other cashback credit cards for the week but for other customers it might have been more of a problem.

When the new card arrived, I signed it immediately. Not in my real name, of course, because I don't want thieves who steal my card to have a copy of my real signature to practice with. I would never sign "David Birch", only fraudsters would do that. But what was puzzling was that that card was, once again, embossed and magnetic striped-up. I don't want either of these fraud vectors on my card. The only place that I would use the stripe is in the USA, and I'm perfectly happy to use other cards while I'm there: in particular my excellent Simple card.

This is all a great waste of everyone's time and money. Until we get a more secure mobile phone-based card infrastructure in place with working tokenisation, can I make a rather obvious suggestion to UK issuers: please block all stripe transactions by default. Customers who want to pay in at-risk areas such as the USA should be required to take special time-limited insecure magnetic stripe cards with them. Surely it would cost my bank less to give me a one-month magnetic stripe-only companion card a couple of times a year than to keep having to reissue chip cards. I would also like the ability to block all CNP transactions with new merchants unless using 3D Secure until my issuer app works properly to confirm transactions.

Incidentally my favourite comment on The Guardian thread was from the chap who said that the US still uses stripe because the NSA finds it easier to read the data and that it's the NSA that is blocking EMV. Sounds plausible to me.

APIs and app stores and the future of banking (6th May)

The lovely people at Finextra kindly invited me along to their FutureMoney event at Level39 in Canary Wharf this year and asked me to moderate the panel about banking app stores, which I loosely interpreted to mean about financial services app stores and APIs. Luckily for me, I had a great panel to work with:

> *Edward Budd from Deutsche Bank, Udayan Goyal from Anthemis Group, David Pope from Jumio, Simon Redfern from Open Bank and Jose Antonio Gallego Vázquez from BBVA.*

[From Finextra: Live: Finextra Future Money, day two][112]

After some initial confusion about the relationship between the colours of the chairs and the colours of the pictures behind them (!) I made a few introductory comments about APIs in this sector and why I felt this was a strategically important discussion.

Following that, we began to examine some of the questions that I had prepared to challenge the panel and brought in questions and observations from the floor to follow. Though I say so myself, it was a terrific session and I would like to broadcast my sincere thanks to the other people who said so too, including Richard Brown from IBM who provided this twestimonial.

A masterclass from @dgwbirch on how to moderate a panel that is both entertaining and informative #FutureMoney

— Richard Gendal Brown (@gendal) May 1, 2014

It was a one-hour session and we were still going strong with questions and debate at the end, which I think is the only effective barometer of both the moderator and the panel. Modesty forbids me from quoting Zilvinas Bareisis of Celent on the session but... oh, wait, no it doesn't...

Given that here both his topic (banking apps and APIs) and panelists were genuinely interesting, it is no surprise that it was perhaps the best session over the two days.

[From CeA "Shout Out" to Finextra Future Money][113]

Richard and Zilvinas are very kind. The reason that the session was such a joy, and was much appreciated by the audience, was that the panelists had exactly right mix of expertise and experience to tackle such a hot topic. I had a bit of an inside track as well, since Consult Hyperion carried out an extensive study of the financial services API world for one of our US customers last year, so I had a pretty good overview of the space in my head to help to shape the discussion. You can read the liveblog for yourself at Finextra, but I want to highlight a couple of what I thought were key points here.

First of all, the importance of the app store and APIs was reinforced. As I said in the introduction, this isn't some obscure technical discussion about parameters and tokens. I think Craig Burton and Steven Willmott capture this nicely with their "Five Axioms of the API Economy". These are:

---

[112] *http://www.finextra.com/news/fullstory.aspx?newsitemid=26021*
[113] *http://bankingblog.celent.com/2014/05/a-shout-out-to-finextra-future-money/*

- Everything and everyone will be API enabled.
- APIs are core to every cloud, social and mobile computing strategy.
- APIs are an economic imperative.
- Organizations must provide their core competence through APIs.
- Organizations must consume core competences of others through APIs.

Secondly, APIs are not all about organisations connecting with other organisations. They are also a way of restructuring the way that bank systems connect internally. This was referred to as "Amazonisation", the idea that every single corporate function should expose its APIs, because other functions within an organisation might be able to do something useful with them. Uday used the excellent example of Fidor Bank as an organisation that has taken those axioms to heart internally.

> We decided from the beginning to build our own middleware, because there was no suitable offer in the market. This is what we now call "Fidor operating system"... fOS is an "open" System. Via standard interfaces we integrate 3rd party offerings into our account.

> *[From FIDOR Bank |]*[114]

In our Consult Hyperion "hot five" for 2014, we highlighted the importance of APIs as part of an electronic transaction strategy and this panel confirmed, to me at least, just how central that API strategy should be to organisational strategies. And they also underlined one of my key messages to our clients: this is business strategy, not technology strategy.

> *Apis are, at their core, not a technical device. Instead, they are a means of delivering or providing access to a service or a product.*

> *[From The Five Axioms of the API Economy, Axiom #3 – Apis are an Economic Imperative | Craig Burton]*[115]

So thanks again to Liz and the rest of the Finextra crowd for giving me the opportunity to learn so much from a terrific panel.

Bank camp (7th July)

The nice people at the Financial Times invited me along to take part in their first "Camp Alphaville" event in London. I took part in a panel

---

[114] *http://jackgavigan.com/2014/05/02/fidor-bank/#comment-916*
[115] *http://www.craigburton.com/?p=3561*

discussion with David Galbraith (a co-founder of Yelp), Jamie Macintosh (Director of the Institute for Security and Resilience at UCL), Sean Park (Anthemis) and the Assistant Governor of the Reserve Bank of Australia, Guy Debelle. The ostensible subject of the discussion was whether the conventional bank model is broken or not, and so I made some notes on the interaction between changes in technology and post-crisis changes in financial services and tried to draw a few conclusions.

How I did this was to build on some work that I've been doing recently for one of our banking clients looking at the technological impact on the different functions within banking. For this I'd used a fairly standard model of banking in the economy, one that divides banking into a number of economic functions and makes the obvious and long-standing observation that while the economy needs these functions to be performed it doesn't necessarily need banks. Therefore the assumption is that the institutional arrangements around these functions will change but that the functions themselves will not. This seems reasonable to me. My key observation was going to be that post-crisis the assumption that some of these core functions such as what economists call the "transfer" functions (savings and loans) and (in particular) the SME lending areas were surrounded by an insurmountable regulatory moat that rendered the banks impervious to competition. However this has turned out not to be the case and technology has introduced new players such as Zopa, Funding Circle and Wonga.

Therefore it seems to me that one way to look at the changing role of the bank is to see it shifting from an organising or directing (or one might even say controlling) role to more of a coordinating role reinforcing what economists call the "incentive functions" around banking, the functions that enable transactions to take place. I imagine I'm a fairly typical middle-class want-to-be saver in the UK market and I already have more money in my Zopa account than I do in my ISA. I can see that in the future my bank might find it more useful and convenient and a means of delivering a better service to me to provide access to my Zopa and my Funding Circle accounts through my banking services and to facilitate transactions between these different kinds of accounts.

If this is even vaguely true then one of the key central coordinating roles of the bank will be to manage the know-your-customer (KYC) and related customer-due-diligence (CDD) issues and to federate identity in a well-defined way between all of the function providers. I tried to sum up this point of view using a conference soundbite that actually got retweeted fairly frequently, not that that necessarily means that I was right, and said that **the bank might shift from being a place where you store your money to being a place where you store your identity**. This is the paradigm shift that I refer to in the title and it reinforces the view that the banking sector as a whole ought to be developing a convincing narrative around identity before it loses even that co-ordinating role.

Anyway, as it happened, we never really got round to talking much about this sort of thing, instead focusing on prostitution and broccoli, because we got a bit side-tracked around cash.

> *Speaking at the Financial Times's Camp Alphaville event, a panel of experts said empirical statistics show that the majority of cash in circulation in places like the UK goes towards funding prostitution, drugs, and tax evasion.*
>
> *[From Physical Cash Economy Propping Up Drugs and Prostitution, say Future of Money Experts]*[116]

But that's the fun of live discussion. Thanks again to Izabella Kaminska at the FT for putting together such a terrific panel for the discussion. I learned a lot.

API Blast (18th Jul)

The organisers of the International Payment Summit 2014 decided to take a little bit of a risk by turning over half of the Day One program to Consult Hyperion for a Future of Money Unconference to explore the subject in an interactive and (hopefully) fun way. So we set off for the Hilton Tower Bridge bright and early on April Fools' Day to test the theory.

As you might have expected, mobile phones and social media were the main technologies that the delegates were discussing and I did learn a lot about different kinds of financial services organisations varying approaches and attitudes, but personally the area of discussion I found most engrossing was around third-party access to bank accounts, the so-called "XS2A" consultation. This is rather a hot topic in Europe because of the European Commission consultations underway in this and related areas.

Forum friend Thaer Sabri, the CEO of the EMA, gave a super presentation on "PSD and third-party access to accounts" that provided a valuable update on the situation. He began by pointing out that the European regulatory landscape, over the last decade or so, hasn't been too constraining and has allowed a reasonable Payment Service Provider (PSP) marketplace to develop and went on to explain how what he called the Technology Service Providers (TSPs) would be developing in the

---

[116] *http://www.ibtimes.co.uk/future-money-experts-physical-cash-only-exists-because-criminal-activity-like-prostitution-1455060*

future as well. In the new Payment Services Directive (PSD2), PSP's will be divided into two categories, as I've written before, so that there will be the Account-Servicing PSP's (ASPs) and the Third-Party PSPs (TPPs). The TPPs come in two flavours: Payment Initiation PSP's (PIPs, that might be someone like Nutmeg) and Account Information PSP's (AIPs, that might someone like Mint).

Thaer went on to talk about some of the additional provisions: that ASPs will be compelled to provide information on funds availability; that PSPs will have to provide a common API under the auspices of the European Banking Authority (EBA) - and we'll be coming back to this "euro-API" in future posts; and that new payment instruments (e.g., decoupled debit) will allow third parties to create payment products on top of that API.

There are, of course, a great many unanswered questions about the legislation, as there always are with this sort of thing, and the answers will shape some aspects of the business model. For example: are end-user contracts sufficient or will TPPs be required to have contracts with banks? And the obvious question of where liability rests in the event of unauthorised transfers, which is the sort of thing that will need to be sorted out before any of this can go anywhere near consumers. Thaer did the audience (and me) a great favour by sketching out some of the likely business impact of these changes and pointed out something that I think is likely to require some significant thoughts on behalf of participants: what is going to happen when bank apps can use the euro-API to access the bank accounts of competitor banks?

A couple of years ago at the Intellect/Payments Council conference, I gave a talk that touched on the "triple A play" strategy of Authentication, Apps and Application Programming Interfaces (APIs) for payment providers and I said that for most people, most of the time, there will be no "payment experience" because the payments will vanish into the apps. David Marcus, who was then President of PayPal, said the same.

> I believe we're heading very quickly toward a new era in which payments will essentially disappear.

> [From State of Payments: Reinventing Money | LinkedIn]

I referred back to this to kick off my talk at the excellent MEETS 2014 conference in Frankfurt. This is the annual event from Sylvia Lukas' PayComm organisation and my once per year opportunity to catch up with payment industry friends from northern, central and eastern Europe. It was as educational, enjoyable and entertaining as always, and for me particularly stimulating this year because of the opportunity to sit in on discussions with banks, schemes, processors and acquirers all developing strategies in response to some significant shifts about to occur in our industry, many of them centred around impending regulatory change. One specific category of interest and importance to our clients is that of the API in banking.

My reason for referring back to my prediction about payments vanishing was to stress the API as the mechanism for it to occur, but then to build on this point to consider the impact of API-centric strategies throughout the payments value chain. It was lucky I'd decided to emphasise the "Amazonisation "of the payments industry in my talk, because the best talk of the event, which was Michael Salmony's (from Equens) opening piece on APIs on the second day, came to similar conclusions from a less technical direction. Michael, as an aside, had the best slide of the entire event, and it wasn't (directly) to do with payments, but was a comment on European standardisation efforts and how they work out in practice!

I must stress that this focus on APIs is not new. It's been clear for some time that this is way forward. I remember from a study on APIs that Consult Hyperion carried out last year for one of our US financial services customers that API-centric strategies make sense - because it's a platform game - whether banks are forced to provide them by the regulators or not.

Moyer cites some banks that are already opening up public APIs, like French banks Crédit Agricole and AXA Bank, and others that have announced plans to do so, like Commonwealth Bank of Australia, ING and Capital One. Overall, she believes there is a growing understanding in the sector of the need for transformation. "I think most banks will provide a public API in the next two years," she says.

[From Banks must focus on APIs and apps, not applications, Siliconrepublic.com][117]

Now, after Michael's excellent talk on the topic, he ran one of the workshop sessions and I was able to join in a fascinating and detailed conversation about the emerging European environment that I commented on in part one of my *API Blast* series of posts.

The EBA (European Banking Authority) is given the task to develop, in close collaboration with the ECB, 'common and secure open standards of communication' (incl. specs for data transmission and how TPPs are to authenticate themselves vis-à-vis AS PSPs). These standards will need a high level of detail and quality (testing) in order to make them usable.

---

[117] *http://www.siliconrepublic.com/strategy/item/29661-interview-banks-must-focus*

[From Access to the Account (XS2A): accelerating the API-economy for banks? | Innopay][118]

I did ask a couple of people what the process for the EBA to develop this API is and what input they are seeking from different stakeholders, but I wasn't able to obtain sufficient clarity to be able to report. Perhaps a correspondent might be able to point me in the right direction?

Anyway, at the workshop session I was in, the delegates were discussing trends in retail payments and they used an interesting classification to drive the debate, exploring how retail payments are changing in all of these areas.

	Cards	**No Cards**
Schemes	the current situation Visa/MC EMV 3DS etc	Visa/MC Euro-API push SCT FPS Zapp Pingit Paym
No Schemes	bilateral	Starbucks prepaid Bitcoin

It's not the point of this blog to report the discussions, but I will say that as far as I could tell, most of the European banks at the event seemed to agree with Michael's point about the importance of developing a strategy around APIs, given the inevitability of the regulatory mandate. There are many aspects to this strategy and, as Craig Burton has said about this, many organisations will have to develop entirely new competencies in order to participate in API-based competition.

> *I think the biggest change is in the area of token and key management. If an organization wants to make sure that its API(s) are not being abused, well managed keys and tokens are essential. Managing developers with keys is probably not something most organizations have ever done.*

[From 1 Raindrop: Security > 140]

A final point with respect to opportunities for banks. There is another way of looking at the strategy around APIs: not centred on payments, but centred on identity. Suppose the bank stored your personal information (rather as was suggested by the SWIFT Innotribe in their work on the digital asset grid, or DAG). Then the API would allow third-parties (and these could be a wide range of organisations, not only PSPSs) controlled access to support recognition, relationships and reputation transactions,

---

[118] *http://www.innopay.com/content/access-account-xs2a-accelerating-api-economy-banks*

reducing the overall costs to the stakeholders while giving the the customer control over their own data via their bank. Could the bank be the ideal partner to implement what Greg Meyer calls "The API of Me":

> *I believe that we as consumers have a right to control the data we share about and between the services and products we use, and that the economic benefit of using and sharing that information by companies should be more transparent. "The API of Me" is the name I'd like to propose for a system of capturing, sharing, and limiting information about consumers*

> *[From The API of Me « Information Maven: Greg Meyer]*

As I said at the Wired Money event, perhaps the role of the bank in the future will change from being a place where you store your money (who keeps their money in a bank these days?) to being a place where you store your identity (surely you'd want to store it with a regulated organisation?).

The wonderful people at ECN invited me to Berlin to give the keynote at their Mobile Payments Innovation Opportunity and Risk conference. My presentation is up on Slideshare if you want to take a look, but I can tell you right now that it wasn't the best presentation at the conference. That was made by Olivier Halluite from Chappuis Halder & Cie, who gave a super overview of the new digital bank experience, delivered a fascinating case study around AXA's mobile first" bank *Soon* and handed out some insightful ideas around the model for services going forward. I'll paraphrase what he said by saying that he saw the implementation of banking functions being hidden and accessed through an identity layer created and owned by Facebook, Apple, Google and such like. He is not alone in seeing a future role for banks as an API that delivers financial services. According to Perficient, and I've got no reason to disagree with them, this kind of "Connected Banking" is one of the top five trends in the financial technology world at the moment.

> *The use of APIs and integration to diversify and advance product offerings is the future of financial services. Innovators at some of the well-established financial institutions are extending access to banking services for developers and partners in today's digital economy to deliver new products and services in the marketplace, personalize experiences, add new mobile services and protect people's privacy through authentication.*

> *[From Top 5 Financial Services Technology Trends – March 2014 | Perficient Financial Services Blog]*

There is a danger that this "connected banking" model turns into a sort of "dumb pipe" model of banking, perhaps as is envisaged by the European

Commission in their consultations around regulated third-party access to bank accounts. This was covered later in the day by our old friend Jean Allix from the Directorate General Competition (DGComp) and his colleague Philippe Pelle from Directorate General Internal Market (DGInt). Ulf Geismar from Edgar Dunn also referred to the "coming wave of regulation" and explained about the opportunities for new entrants to come into the payment space to compete in a fair playing field.

I couldn't resist asking, though, whether it really will be a fair playing field. Going back to the Olivier's presentation, if the banks are essentially condemned to a future as utility pipes that are mandated to provide a "euro-API" for third parties including the "OTTs" who have the relationship with the customer (and all the value-added services and profits), then they better have some plans to become operationally-efficient pipes otherwise they will be accumulated and agglomerated.

Naturally, this leads me to speculate what this will mean specifically for payments. If anyone can initiate payments through the API, then won't the fascist nature of monopoly capitalism shape the new business environment? How is opening up the market to competition going to help if the market is then dominated by (e.g.) Facebook and Apple instead of Visa and MasterCard? This cannot be what the Commission intends, but I am curious to know what other outcomes people are imagining. It could be that retailers and service providers take the initiative themselves and access bank account directly, for example.

I'm sure this won't happen, of course, because I imagine that Visa and MasterCard are right now developing strategies for new push products that will sit on the euro-API and make it easy for merchants to accept new, lost-cost, hard-token, debit-lite payments.

A suggestion for doing something about account switching in the UK (12th October)

BBC Moneybox is a fixed point in my week. It's a window for us fintech types to peer through to look into the kitchens of ordinary consumers the length and breadth of the country. It's a really good way of understanding the real issues that people see in dealing with a variety of financial services organisations and therefore provides constant inspiration as to where new kinds of products and services might be built around new technology to improve things for all.

I happened to be listening to a recent episode when the issue of current account switching in the UK was raised. For those of you who haven't been following the story, some time ago the British government forced the banks here to spend an enormous amount of money on a system to speed up the switching of current accounts because in 2011 the Independent Commission on Banking (ICB) wanted to make it easier for customers to change from bank to bank and therefore to increase competition in the retail banking sector.

Switching bank accounts became quicker and simpler following the introduction of new 'faster switching' rules in September 2013.

[From Switching bank accounts - how to find the best current account deals | This is Money][119]

Oddly, neither the ICB nor the Payments Council asked for my opinion — which was to look at portability — and instead decided to build a big computer system to shift payments and so forth between bank accounts. The system, known as the current account switch service (CASS), was complicated and expensive, as big computer systems generally are.

Experts were impressed with the scheme, which has cost £750m.

[From More bank account switching? The number has actually fallen - Telegraph][120]

I wasn't. A year ago, I took part in a CSFI roundtable discussion about the system and I think I may have annoyed some of the people present by maintaining that the system was pointless and wouldn't make any difference.

October 16, 2013. The impact of current account switching on UK retail banking: A round-table discussion with Adrian Kamellard (Payments Council), Niamh Grogan (Lloyds Banking Group), Ashleye Gunn (Which?), David Parker (Accenture) and Dave Birch (Consult Hyperion).

I also said it was a waste of time and money, a pointless political posture that would not make the slightest difference to competition in the retail banking sector. I wasn't saying this from any kind of ideological perspective but from an examination of the facts on the ground.

So three-quarters of the populace were satisfied with the current system? It currently takes two to three weeks to switch bank

---

[119] http://www.thisismoney.co.uk/money/saving/article-1585173/Switching-bank-accounts-best-current-account-deals.html
[120] http://www.telegraph.co.uk/finance/personalfinance/bank-accounts/11092982/More-bank-account-switching-The-number-has-actually-fallen.html

accounts in the UK, but later this month it will take only a week. Who cares?

[From Do pointless things, faster - Tomorrow's Transactions]^{121}

Now we are a year on, the numbers are in, the results are unequivocal. The number of people switching bank accounts has actually gone down. Some uncharitable persons, of whom I am not one, will undoubtably observe that a billion or so quid for a new computer system that makes things worse is actually run-of-the-mill for government-directed IT spending and an inevitable consequence of the combination of well-meaning but technologically illiterate politicians and IT vendors but I think this a harsh judgement.

In recent days news has arrived that the Financial Conduct Authority (FCA) has launched an investigation into the service but they seem to have added a little bit of special sauce, hopefully because of some of my old blog posts…

The Current Account Switch Service is not the only option to make switching easier for current account customers. Alongside our review of the new service we will also gather evidence on other options including account number portability (ANP).

[From Current Account Switch Service - Financial Conduct Authority]^{122}

Yes, they are going to take another look at portability. I have a vague suspicion that there are still people who think that account numbers are a bit like mobile phone numbers (which they are not[123]) and so they are about to waste another couple of billion quid on a system that will allow you to take your account number from one bank to another. I hope they'll ask me about this as part of their review, because there is an obvious way forward that doesn't involve spending gazillions on management consultants and big iron.

First of all let's recapitulate the central point. If people could keep their account number, while moving the actual account from one financial institution to another, it would undoubtedly make it faster (in fact, instantaneous) to switch accounts and might be a factor in increasing

---

[121] *http://tomorrowstransactions.com/2013/09/do-pointless-things-faster/*
[122] *http://www.fca.org.uk/about/what/promoting-competition/current-account-switch*
[123] *http://tomorrowstransactions.com/2011/05/could-bank-account-numbers-be-portable-like-mobile-numbers/*

competition. I doubt that what consumers say about this is actually any indication of future behaviour, but for what it's worth...

Consumers would be more likely to switch their bank if they could keep their account number, according to new Which? research... Three-quarters (76%) believe that the introduction of portable account numbers would make switching bank accounts easier... More than half of the people surveyed (55%) have never switched their current account.

[From Keeping bank account number would boost switching say consumers - September - 2012 - Which? News]

So. What should we do? Well, as I have bored people to tears with at length repeatedly over a period of some years, what we should do is use virtual account numbers. I wrote two years ago what the industry should have done, which is to create a virtual sort code and account number that customers can switch to wherever they like: that way, they give their employers and whoever else a single sort code and account number which never, ever changes, Then, if they want to switch bank, they re-route the virtual account and there's no need to notify billers, counter parties etc to update their databases[124].

Let's call this a VAN. A virtual account number. Now, you know how all mobile phone numbers in the UK begin with a "7". Well, what if all virtual account numbers in the UK began with "7" as well? It turns out that the "7" sort codes in the UK have an unusual history...

Individual sort codes within the range 70-00-00 to 70-99-99 were allocated on a one-off basis to the many London offices of private and foreign banks... By the 1990s, all these banks had been issued with sort codes within the ranges of the various clearing banks which, henceforth, acted as clearing agents for them... and use of the 70 code range was discontinued.

[From Sort code - Wikipedia, the free encyclopedia]

That's right. The 70 code is unused, so we can issue people with VANs of the form 70-ZX-XX 99999999. These would be compatible with all existing systems and with the IBAN scheme. I suggest that we use that "Z" in the VAN as a good old-fashioned check digit, leaving 11 digits for the individual account numbers, making a "70 solution" for ANP that is feasible with no impact on existing systems. I think it would be rather fun to have all mobile phone numbers starting with a "7" and all mobile bank account numbers starting with a "70".

---

[124] http://tomorrowstransactions.com/2012/10/e-ass-about-face/

As there are less than 100 million bank accounts in the UK, the scheme provides multiple VANs for each person, business, charity, government department and so on in the UK, which ought to be adequate for the foreseeable future, and could be kickstarted with absolutely no effort by consumers at all. The initial database mapping the virtual account numbers to the real account numbers can be created in an overnight run by the banks exporting all current account numbers to the virtual account number system. Then consumers could use their home banking authentication to log in to the virtual account number system (with the obvious acronym VANS) to "claim" their VAN by adding their relevant contact details, such as a mobile phone number and email address, and more importantly to change the target account number whenever they wanted. The system might even reserve a few vanity VANs like 7X-XX-XX 00000007 or 7X-99-99 87654321 or 7X-99-99 99999999 for auction to the highest bidder to help fund the system.

Having lots of VANs is useful. I might have a work VAN and a home VAN, for example. My wife and I might decide to have three VANs: one that maps to our joint account and one each to map to our individual savings accounts. When opening a new bank account, consumers would be asked whether they wanted to use an existing VAN or create a new one: the new VAN would be created or the existing VAN directed to the new account there and then.

An obvious extension of the VAN scheme would be to allow consumers to direct payments to the mobile phone number or e-mail address registered against the VAN, thus providing the functionality of PingIt and PayM but at a more general level. You might even allow consumers when claiming a VAN for the first time to choose a "Payment Name" for that VAN, just as they choose a Twitter name or a Facebook name... Now that's an idea.

Push payments are a win-win (and a lose) (1st July)

The "Push Payments Manifesto" at OpenPayee echoes my views on the long-term evolution of the retail payments sector precisely. I've written beforeabout how effective push payments will displace other mechanisms, and the manifesto identifies the core reason why.

> *Payments made using any form of identity token which gives the payee the ability to pull the payment out of the payer's account are bad.*

> *[From Push Payments Manifesto | OpenPayee]*

Quite. And as the manifesto points out, pull payments are a relic from the bygone past when consumers did not have devices and there was no network to connect them to. Now that there is a network and there are smart devices connected to it, there's no need for these dated hacks. To illustrate the point, as I did at the BayPay London meeting recently, consider the prosaic (and in my case entirely hypothetical) example of gym membership.

Right now, this system "works" through continuous authorities (CAs) on cards. And, as we all know, these are nothing but hassle. If you've ever tried to stop someone from taking money from your card once you've given them an authority, you'll know what I mean. People often find that the only way to do it is to cancel their card and switch issuer!

Now consider the modern alternative. You are walking down the street and a message pops up on your phone: it's your Barclays app telling you that the gym have requested their monthly tenner. (Is this about right? I have no idea what gyms cost.) You put your thumb on your iPhone fingerprint reader to OK the transaction and go about your day. Meanwhile in the background there is an FPS transfer to the gym account and about one second later they have their money. Now, you probably wouldn't want to be bothered with this kind of payment trivia all day long, so I expect that you would set your Barclays app to auto-OK future payments to the gym within certain bounds. So actually, when walking down the street you would simply see a message on your phone telling you that the gym membership had been paid. Now, when you want to cancel your gym membership, you just tell your Barclays app to auto-decline instead. Sorted. Better for the customer, and better for the bank too.

Bill payment represents the biggest monthly cost on a checking account, by a wide margin (OK, maybe debit processing costs might be more, but that's offset by revenue

[From Is Bill Payment Dead and Gone in Five Years? « Gonzobanker.com][125]

This might be a weapon for banks to regain some of their lost ground in billing while simultaneously improving service to customers by given them more control over payments.

The percentage of online and mobile payments made on biller sites increased from 62% in 2010 to 69% in 2013. Bank site payments declined from 38% of online/mobile bills paid to 30% (with third-party sites like Check.com picking up 2%) over the same period.

---

[125] *http://www.gonzobanker.com/2014/05/bill-pay-dead-and-gone/*

[From Banks Are Losing The Online Bill Pay Game | Snarketing 2.0][126]

How exactly this will work, however, obviously depends on the infrastructure available for the banks and billers to use. In the US, this means that people tend to think about ACH.

If I were at a bank right now, I'd take my fresh, new business intelligence system and identify all of my customers who use bill pay to make regular payments to utilities, phone companies and the like. Then, I'd start a campaign to get them from bill pay to biller-initiated ACH.

[From Is Bill Payment Dead and Gone in Five Years? « Gonzobanker.com]

I don't think this is the only architecture. Given the combination of smart phones, advances in mutual recognition and the reduced management costs of push payments, surely a more likely path is for the biller to message the customer and have the customer respond by initiating a push payment across an immediate settlement network (such as FPS in the UK). It's a win-win (except for the gym).

It's, like, how much more white could this be? (28th November)

There is a particular kind of attack on EMV that works because the cryptographic data of a certain kind ("cryptograms") generated by certain kinds of cards are not properly checked when they wend their way back to the issuing bank.

(Please note that this attack does not work with UK issued cards, or at least cards issued by UK issuers who have the right consultants, and hasn't worked here for many years.)

The cryptograms aren't checked properly for, by and large, one of two reasons. It's either because the bank hasn't installed the necessary hardware and software to do it properly (this sometimes happens because they are pushed into issuing but don't have the budget or time to do things correctly) or the bank does have the necessary infrastructure but the operations people get the IT people to ignore the cryptogram check as customers are getting annoyed with transactions being declined.

---

[126] *http://snarketing2dot0.com/2013/09/17/banks-are-losing-the-online-bill-pay-game/*

The Tomorrow's Transactions Reader 2015

(Please don't bother sending me emails about these points because I know the statements are gross oversimplifications!)

Anyway, on with the story.

Many years ago, when my colleagues at Consult Hyperion were testing this sort of thing in the UK, we used to make our own EMV cards. To do this, we essentially took valid card data and loaded it onto our own Java cards. These are what we in the business call white plastic, because they are a white plastic card with a Java card chip on it but otherwise completely blank

Since the white plastic card could not generate the correct cryptogram (because you can't get the necessary key out of the chip on the real card), we just set the cryptogram value to be "SDA ANTICS" or whatever (in hex).

You might call these cards pseudo-clones. They act like clones in that they work correctly in the terminals, but they are not real clones because they don't have the right keys inside them. Naturally, if you make one of these pseudo-clones, you don't want to be bothered with PIN management so you make it into what is called a "yes card". That is, you instead of programming the chip to check that the correct PIN is entered, you programme it to respond "yes" to whatever PIN is entered.

It's one of our campfire stories that I got into a lot of trouble once with one of the UK issuing banks because I once thought it would be cute to demonstrate our EMV chops with one of these cards.

I had a new card issued to me. When the PIN mailer arrived I didn't open it. We made a clone of the card as a "yes card" and I used it to buy a train ticket to go up to a meeting at the bank. When we got to the bank I showed them the train ticket, the POS receipt showing that the card had been used and the PIN verified, the card and the unopened PIN mailer. I thought they would think this was interesting and would immediately hire the right consultants to help them sort out their issuing strategy. Instead, they got really upset with me because it meant they had to stop card issuing and go to the marketing persons and explain to them why one of their favourite projects was going on ice. Oh well.

The reason I'm telling you this yonks old stuff about the early days of EMV is that in some countries these problems, the problems associated with certain kinds of cryptograms not being checked, still exist and I just heard a terrific first-hand story about this from a pal. He discovered that a particular bank in a particular country was issuing the particular kind of card that could be vulnerable to this kind of attack and he wanted to find out whether the bank was actually checking cryptograms properly (they weren't). In order to determine this he made a pseudo-clone card. He programmed it as a "yes card" and went into a shop to try it out.

When he put the completely blank white card into the terminal, the shopkeeper asked him what he was doing and what the completely blank white card was. My pal, thinking quickly, told him that it was one of the new Apple credit cards. "Cool" said the shopkeeper, "How can I get one?".

What is the right innovation paradigm for banking? (3rd December)

In the opening talk at this year's NetFinance Interactive, Vince Hruska of City National Bank made the very good point that innovation in banking is harder (for a variety of reasons) than innovation in a whole range of other areas and focused on mobile as an area where you see innovation and growth has been outside of banks (he used Venmo as an example) and he left me wondering how exactly banks will change their structures when they have an elephant in the vault.

Here's what I mean. There was a special feature on the future of banking in the July 2014 edition of *Prospect* magazine. The Director of Strategy at the British Bankers' Assocation, James Barty, said that banks have to innovate, otherwise competitors will eat away at their business (which I'm sure we would all agree with) and that the biggest innovation challenge facing the banks is their own legacy IT infrastructure.

I'm sure he is right about this. Legacy infrastructure is a huge problem. But legacy thinking is too. I remember a depressing but accurate, comment on this from Erin McClure at Glenbrook that framed a particular aspect of this problem.

> *The revolving door of leadership between banks and their solution providers doesn't help.*

> *[From Co-Dependence Between Banks and Their Technologists: Hampering Innovation — Payments Views from Glenbrook Partners]*

I'm convinced that the only way to bring real innovation into the finance sector is by separating the lines of business. In particular, we should pull payments away from the bank and both the payments business and the banking business will benefit. Let new people have a go at payments. Let new people look at the areas of payments that are not systemically-risky and try to work in entirely new ways. The payment systems we are familiar with, such as card payments and direct debits, date back to a time before the internet and mobile phones. They are remnants of an antediluvian ecosystem, ill-suited to the new climate and destined for extinction.

This doesn't help the core banking business. Despite all of their labs and accelerators and incubators, the focus of their spending remains the legacy infrastructure. So this makes me wonder what the cross-over point is; where it no longer makes sense to keep patching up the legacy infrastructure and instead just chuck it (and Erin's "military-industrial complex" that comes with it) and start again.

If we did start again, one of the things we (i.e., the industry) might do differently is change the focus of innovation. Back in 2012, Nasir Zubari wrote that banks were being "selfish" with innovation, in the sense that their view of innovation is shaped by the hard statistics. He said that out of the 64 million bank accounts in the UK, less than 0.1%, had voted with their feet and shifted banking provider in the four years to the end of 2011, and even then they were shifting to another bank providing essentially the same service as the one they left. This set the dynamic for innovation.

> *For specific services at the consumer and SME level, banks rarely bother with improving services and incurring R&D expense. Why should they? They are not going lose nor gain any customers regardless.*

> *The fact that 1) banks don't share their innovation benefits with customers 2) banks can avoid innovation in services altogether, spawns opportunity for innovators to do the opposite. Welcome the "New Finance" sector.*

> *[From Nasir Zubairi: Selfish Shylocks]*

Maybe this is the right structure. Maybe what Nasir called the "new finance" sector or what we call the "fintech" sector should be doing the innovation that shares benefits between stakeholders. It is at least a plausible hypothesis that banks innovate to make themselves more efficient, while supporting innovation from non-banks and near-banks (look at the case studies of Simple and Moven, for example) to deliver new products and services. Matt Harris framed this new business perspective very well, saying that:

> *In 10 years, I suspect that these lines will have entirely diverged, as the banks become relatively stable financial utilities, their vendors settle into a symbiotic but unexciting and slow upgrade and refresh cycle and the Finsurgents complete their takeover of customer facing applications and innovation in the sector.*

> *[From Redefining FinTech | Finsurgency]*

I made a note of these comments from Nasir and Matt a couple of years ago because they fit with an API-based approach to services that we were looking at for one of our US financial services customers and reviewing them now I think they provide a decent paradigm for linking the technology roadmap with the bigger picture around the banking business. It's about banks helping others to share.

Chapter 9: Retail and Transport

Anyone can invent a new payment mechanism, it's easy (or at least it's easy if you know how!). Getting a new payment mechanism accepted, that's the hard part. For the average person throughout the whole world, retail and transport are the places where they spend their money, not on the web or in the cloud, and these are the points-of-sale where innovation needs traction.

The "hot five" retail transaction technologies for 2014 (2nd January)

First, some background as to why I started thinking about this topic and ended up with my shortlist of five. A couple of weeks back, as Richard Watson mentioned on his excellent "What's Next" blog, we had a bit of a catch up, talking about the major trends in and around the technologies, businesses and social memes that we are interested in.

> *Or it could it be the rather relaxed lunch I had with Dave Birch talking about Bitcoin, identity and steak.*
>
> *[From Just stuff | What's Next: Top Trends][127]*

We did have a relaxed lunch, it's true. Richard is a futurist, and the author of The Future Files, which he kindly came and talked about at our Forum a couple of years ago and in a rather spooky coincidence he emailed me about something while I actually had a copy of his book on my desk! I had been looking up something for a book I am writing. But back to lunch.

I'm going to be helping Richard update the financial services route on his roadmap (which is what he's looking at in the restaurant in the picture) and we were discussing the long-term significance of Bitcoin and the Bitcoin family of technologies. Richard set me thinking about ways to provide useful input to his roadmap. In our internal roadmap, the one we use to support clients in developing their product and service roadmaps, we divide technology evolution into "now" (1-2 years), "soon" (3-5 years) and "later" (5+ years). One way of using this roadmap is to see business as a way of connecting the technology push and the social pull to deliver sustainable value. With this framing, I looked at the technologies that are reaching the mass market now and that gave me a short list. Then I went and asked around a few of our guys. Since they are, by and large, out working for clients (who are some of the biggest and most important players in the retail transactions space) and since, by and large, they are

---

[127] *http://toptrends.nowandnext.com/2013/12/03/just-stuff/*

working on projects around exploring the latest technologies, they are a pretty good barometer.

So, by combining projects that we are working on now with the likely business impact of the technologies, taking away the projects that are confidential (!) and focusing on technologies likely to be of interest to blog readers, I got my "hot five" technologies for 2014! I'm genuinely interested in your feedback on my picks, which are…

Proximity and vicinity interfaces. The arrival of Host Card Emulation (HCE) and Bluetooth Low Energy (BLE) will open up mobile transactions, taking them away from (expensive) secure, controlled infrastructure and out into the open. While security and risk analysis skills will be crucial to delivering operational systems, I think that the overall mobile security environment means that there will be a revolution in app-centric retail. I can well imagine using NFC to "tap in" to Waitrose before being guided around by BLE and then a "tap out" to close and pay. See if you can spot the BLE beacon in this photograph of our CTO hard at work down at CHYP End…

Tokenisation. This made the front pages later in the year when the major payment schemes made it a priority and I suppose it was given an end-of-year boost because of the Target breach. I'll blog about it soon, but one of the key points in the coverage to date is that Target's own tokenised product was safe from the hackers whereas the untokenised general-purpose card numbers were not. This reinforced the schemes' determination to make a serious dent in online fraud by moving away from cardholder PANs as the key to payments.

> *Visa, MasterCard and American Express have announced a proposed framework for a new global standard to enhance the security of digital payments and simplify the purchasing experience when shopping on a mobile phone, tablet, personal computer or other smart device.*

> *[From MasterCard, Visa and American Express Propose New Global Standard to Make Online and Mobile Shopping Simpler and Safer][128]*

This has been reported as being a technology initiative that undermines NFC, whereas I tend to think that it dovetails with it.

---

[128] http://www.paymentsnews.com/2013/10/mastercard-visa-and-american-express-propose-new-global-standard-to-make-online-and-mobile-shopping-simpler-and-safer.html

My two cents is that this finally puts the stake in the heart of NFC by those who started the whole thing in the first place.

[From 2013 - Networks, The Cloud And Many Open Questions | PYMNTS.com®][129]

As I said at the time, I'm not sure I agree with Karen about this because there is a positive synergy between tokenisation and proximity interfaces that is mutually beneficial. Tokens don't need the same kind of security that card details do so they can thrive in the HCE/BLE-driven app.

Recognition. We've been using the word "recognition" to mean the combination of *good enough* identification and *good enough* *authentication* to make commerce possible. The mobile phone has an obvious and important role to play here, to the point where downstream tokenisation will shift to recognition (in other words, it will be the customer's identity that is used to make a payment). I continue to think that making privacy part of the consumer proposition here will be a good strategy. It also seems to me that the tools for creating recognition infrastructure at reasonable cost are becoming standardised (FIDO, OpenIDConnect, OIX, that sort of thing) so organisations will want to use them on a large scale. HCE/BLE give us the convenient interfaces, tokenisation protects privacy and customers benefit from a personalised experience.

2014 will be the year in which you walk into a store and it "knows you" and customizes your visit.

[From Predictions for 2014: Computing Technologies In The Age Of The Customer | Forrester Research]

Small Data. With all the talk about Big Data, I think there is an opportunity for "small data" to make a difference. Giving customers their own data and the tools to manage it seems to me to be a way to balance individual and organisational wants. The relevance of this to payments and identity plays is that the "wallet" of whatever form becomes a place to store and manage this small data — consumer receipts and warranties, spending history, loyalty and so on — as well as the tools that consumers can use to manage that data to their benefit. I saw a nice comment about this in response to Robert X. Cringley's call for 2014 predictions:

2014 could benefit from a renewed focus on delivering value by sorting out the small data first.

---

[129] http://www.pymnts.com/briefing-room/commerce-3-0/open-platforms-and-the-cloud/2013/Networks-The-Cloud-And-Many-Open-Questions

[From I, Cringely Call for 2014 predictions! - I, Cringely]

APIs. The glue that holds all of this together. There is no doubt about the crucial role of APIs in the future business architecture, but what will change in 2014 is that APIs have become a management issue, not a technology issue. I'm fascinated by the nature of API-based competition, but for our clients (who tend to be at the larger end of the scale) the fact that they can start to compete on the basis of APIs is problematic because they have no experience of competing in that way. It's been a while since the Credit Agricole app store (the CAStore) became the first post-modern (!) bank app and the floodgates haven't opened yet, but when Consult Hyperion studied financial services APIs for one of our international clients earlier in the year one of the clear conclusions of the work was that APIs will increasingly shape the products and services that are delivered through them.

> *The CAStore uses an open API, or application programming interface, in which technology is shared freely with outside developers so that it can be integrated into new programs, without compromising compatibility.*
>
> *[From Open API for Bank Apps: Can Credit Agricole s Model Work Here? - American Banker Magazine Article][130]*

When we are helping clients to put together their technology roadmaps we try to find ways for business to link the push of new technology with the pull of social change to identify new products and services in the secure electronic transactions world. I think these five technologies form the basis for a consistent narrative for retail transactions in response to real customer requirements for convenience, security and value. I can't wait for the next version of my Waitrose app!

The real wallet wars are about to begin (9th January)

When I was putting together a few slides on the future of electronic wallets for one of our clients, I thought I would start by lining up a heavy hitter on my side to help convince corporate middle management that wallets are a serious topic and are worth investing time and money in.

> *Microsoft (MSFT) will introduce its own version of "wallet" software for electronic commerce, but the company does not intend to compete with Internet payment firms, an executive said today. "We are creating a wallet that will allow payment*

---

[130] http://www.americanbanker.com/magazine/123_8/open-api-for-bank-apps-can-credit-agricoles-model-work-1060535-1.html

companies to plug in their payment systems," said Jonathan Weinstein, Microsoft group product manager... "Wallet" software contains a buyer's payment methods for purchases on the Net, such as credit card numbers, electronic cash, digital IDs, and electronic checks.

[From <u>Microsoft to open digital wallet - CNET News</u>][131]

Sounds pretty interesting, until you notice that the article is dated 26th March 1997. Seventeen years ago. I'm not picking on Microsoft, I'm just using them as an example. They;re actually doing some interesting work in the wallet world. Last year, one of Consult Hyperion's top software developer chaps wrote about his experiences at the <u>Microsoft Digital Wallet Foundry</u> in London, working on software for the Microsoft Windows Phone wallet.

The purpose of the Digital Wallet Foundry events is to inspire disruptive ideas about digital wallets in a variety of sectors, and to encourage those ideas to be developed into demonstrators or proof of concepts.

[From <u>Hammering out an app at the Digital Wallet Foundry</u>][132]

He built a great app, as did others at the event. But I still don't have a digital wallet that stores my debit card, my driving licence and my bus ticket. Why is this all taking so long? Why don't I have a mobile wallet on my iPhone right now, from Microsoft or from anyone else? Why did I have to type in my name, address, card number, expiry date and security code into the travel ticketing application that I used this morning?

Payments players with digital wallet aspirations — including Visa, MasterCard, Google, PayPal, Apple and Isis — are all vying for customers' virtual pocket books in a race to truly electronic transactions. Yet none have had much luck, so far.

[From <u>Digital Wallet Race Is Far From Over - American Banker Article</u>][133]

The truth is that almost all of the payments that I make with my mobile — recently these have included car parking (RingGo), taxi (Hailo), coffee

---

[131] *http://news.cnet.com/Microsoft-to-open-digital-wallet/2100-1017_3-278317.html*
[132] *http://www.chyp.com/media/blog-entry/hammering-out-an-app-at-the-digital-wallet-foundry*
[133] *http://www.americanbanker.com/issues/178_66/digital-wallet-race-is-far-from-over-1058114-1.html*

(Barclaycard OnePulse), bus (Arriva) and my eldest son (Barclays Mobile Banking) -- are made using "domain-centric" apps, not payment apps. And what is central to these apps is me. For several of these transactions, I don't even know how I paid. I can't remember which cards or accounts I registered or selected and I don't really want to be bothered about this when I'm doing something like getting on a bus. So long as it's only me that can use the app, the payment mechanism is essentially uninteresting. Identity is, as they say, the new money. If you are wondering who "they" are people like... well, there's me, of course, but there are also important and influential people, like Jack.

> *"It's not about payment," Jack Dorsey, a founder of Square, a PayPal competitor, says. "It's about identity. And it's about the experience that a merchant can create, which is what actually builds loyalty. We believe that it's important that the technology, the mechanics of payments, actually fade away to the background."*

> *[From EBay's Strategy for Taking On Amazon - NYTimes.com]*

If we're going to get somewhere with wallets, we need to change our view of wallets. Maybe wallet is an infrastructure built around what we at Consult Hyperion have taken to calling **recognition**, not an application built around what we have for a long time called payments. As I said a couple of years ago,

> *The impending wallet wars are about more than control over the consumers' payments, they are about control over identity.*

> *[From You searched for wallet identity - Tomorrow's Transactions]*

That's why the tactics around wallets are switching this year and you'll be reading more and more about the real competition in the wallet world: not between Visa and MasterCard or between Barclays and Lloyds, but between banks and Facebook, telecommunications operators and Apple, retailers and Google..

Retailers could take more advantage of contactless (5th February)

Contactless is growing and it is starting to have an impact.

> *Transport for London (TfL) has today announced that it is to stop accepting cash fares on London buses from summer this year.*

The Tomorrow's Transactions Reader 2015

[From London buses to go cashless from mid 2014 | Transport for London][134]

But as yet we are nowhere near, say, Australia. Down under, they have 175,000+ contactless POS terminals and the contactless limit is already $100 (it's still £20 back in Blighty). The biggest mobile operator (Telstra) already has more than a million NFC handsets on its network and the numbers are still going up. So we're not at Oz levels yet, or possibly even Canadian levels, where the contactless "no PIN" limit has also been raised to $100 without apparent ill effect and there are contactless terminals in all of the main retailers.

In Australia, six in ten Visa and MasterCard supermarket transactions are contactless. Some retailers there want to install contactless-only terminals (this is currently against scheme rules AFAIK). We are nowhere near that in the UK. Visa's top contactless market in Europe is Poland. I'm convinced that one of the reasons that our contactless take up has been slower is that retailers don't really seem to know what to do with it. It baffles me that some retailers ban you from paying with cards for transactions below £10 when it would be more logical for them to say that transactions below £10 **must** be contactless.

At least Subway have a sign which allows you to pay by contactless for any value but has a minimum spend for [chip and PIN] credit and debit.

[From You searched for greggs - Tomorrow's Transactions]

This came up again when I went to Brighton recently. I went to a very trendy coffee shop with a guest and ordered a couple of coffees and a cake. It came to a fiver or so. Naturally, I didn't have any cash so I opened my no.2 wallet (the domestic travel wallet) and took out a contactless payment card. The lady behind the counter took the card from me, told me it was an extra 60p for card payments (if it had said that on the door I would have gone somewhere else) and put it in the slot, but I could see that the terminal she was using had a contactless interface. So I explained to her that the coincidence of my having one of the 36+ million contactless cards in the UK and her having one of the 164,000+ contactless terminals meant that it would save her money by using contactless. So I got her to cancel the transaction and then rekey it so that I could tap. Which I did. And having made my contactless payment with a theatrical flourish and tap, I told her that one of the additional advantages of contactless was that it saves time. She fixed me with a steely glare and said "it hasn't so far". I am a stranger in a strange land.

---

[134] *http://www.tfl.gov.uk/corporate/media/newscentre/29557.aspx*

Ian Cranna, VP Marketing and Category at Starbucks UK… "The introduction of contactless has had a real benefit for all our customers, whether they pay with contactless or not, as it cuts waiting time in the line.

[From <u>Saving time with contactless | /review - Gemalto</u>][135]

Contrast this experience with the Platform 2 coffee chap at Woking station. Most days, I have a coffee at home before I amble off to catch the 7.59 Flying Glacier to Waterloo via all points beyond mobile coverage between West Byfleet and Vauxhall. But maybe once a week I'll be doing stuff or be running late and I'll grab a coffee at the station. When I do, I prefer to go to the Platform 2 coffee chap as I think his coffee is slightly nicer than the Starbucks on Platform 1 or the store on Platform 2. But I also love the raisin danish that he does. But I never have any money. So in the old days, that meant no sale because I would go to Starbucks and use my mobile app instead (and not get the raisin danish that I want). Then they got a POS terminal so you could pay with chip and PIN, which works fine, but obviously there can be a bit of a line at peak times. Last week I went to the coffee chap and asked for a latte and a raisin danish and sleepily handed over a contactless Visa card. He tapped it on his contactless terminal and gave it back to me.

Wow. Better for him, better for me and better for everyone else in the queue behind me. The only thing that would make it even better would be to take the contactless antenna off of his POS terminal and put it on the counter so that I don't have to hand him my card or my phone or my watch in order to pay. Nevertheless, I thought this excellent payment experience could not go unremarked.

I was so shocked I didn't recover until the trackside fire at Wandsworth.

Loyalty points are money (11th[th] March)

It is not unusual to hear people at conferences about payments (e.g., me) talk about loyalty points and say that they are already a form of money, which is sort of true. The concrete proof that they are form of money is that people steal them. Remember the proliferation of recent stories about Tesco loyalty points being the subject of widespread attack.

Tesco customers have complained that vouchers worth hundreds of pounds have disappeared from their online rewards accounts, raising the possibility that thieves hacked into the company's system.

---

[135] *http://review.gemalto.com/post/saving-time-with-contactless*

[From Tesco calls in police after dozens of customers complain that their Clubcard accounts have been emptied online | Mail Online][136]

In case you were wondering where these stolen loyalty points are going to, well...

Screengrabs taken from Silk Road 2, the successor to the original site, reveal that its most popular items for sale until recently were Tesco Clubcard vouchers. Vouchers worth £100 each, offered by a vendor using the handle Revivalry, were selling for $61 (£43).

[From Silk Road website did roaring trade in Tesco Clubcard vouchers | Society | The Observer][137]

Seriously: last weekend, the most popular items for sale on the darkest of dark webs, the spawn of Bitcoin and Satan, Silk Road, were Tesco vouchers. Not terrorist training manuals, ketamine samplers or child porn DVDs, but Tesco vouchers. In other words, money. Sold at a discount. And a pretty big discount (not that I know what money launderers generally charge for this sort of thing). Pound notes selling for 43p.

Yes, these vouchers are money. As I've written before, a John Lewis voucher, a Clubcard voucher, a Marks & Spencer's voucher, are all means of exchange that trade at par. I have personal experience of this and will state unequivocally that I will accept John Lewis vouchers as de facto legal tender for the discharge of debits incurred. I spend a fortune at Amazon, so Amazon e-vouchers are money. Anywhere I spend money, there is the potential for a money substitute. Surely this is where e-money is taking us.

When I was originally mulling over the threats to supermarkets throughout the land, I heard a report on BBC Radio about the Metropolitan Police calling for something to be done about ticket fraud for pop concerts and sporting events, running at about £40m per annum in London, if I heard correctly.

The Metropolitan Police's specialist ticket fraud unit has called on the government to introduce legislation around the resale of tickets to gigs and sports events.

---

[136] *http://www.dailymail.co.uk/news/article-2280897/Tesco-calls-police-dozens-customers-complain-Clubcard-accounts-emptied-online.html*
[137] *http://www.theguardian.com/society/2014/mar/09/silk-road-website-roraring-trade-tesco-vouchers*

[From BBC - Newsbeat - Police call for ticket resale legal regulation][138]

This is ludicrous. It is absurd that ticketing reselling is illegal at all, If you bought a ticket, you should be entitled to do what you like with it. But that's by-the by. The source of these problems are the same as the source of the loyalty points problems and most other fraud problems: As you might expect, the lack of an identity infrastructure. Identity is the money, but it's also the new loyalty card, the pop concert ticket and the sporting event ticket.

Receipts are a way to make wallets better (18th May)

We all understand that if we are going to replace the leather wallet with a digital one, it's got to do a lot more than payments. Korea's second largest mobile operator, KT, know this and so when they launched a new m-payment system "MoCa" they were part of the package. They also kicked off the "The MoCa Alliance", which has already brought on board over 60 companies including the country's leading banking institutions, coffee shop chains, and department stores.

> *[Interview : Shim Kyu-young, Seoul Resident] "I didn't like that my wallet was thick due to cards, receipts, and coupons. Now my wallet is thin and it's nice that I can comfortably use my smartphone."*

> *[From Arirang News]*

This may have lost something in translation, but you get the point. Making payments electronic only gets us part of the way to the digital wallet. We need to make everything else electronic as well and the rather obvious place to start is the receipt, something of a weak link. A typical modern payment experience, for me, involves tapping a card or a phone on a reader for a transaction that takes a couple of hundred milliseconds and then standing around waiting for a printer to chunter out a paper receipt that I don't actually want anyway. There must be a better way, and Walmart is trying one.

> *The retailer will identify the consumer by asking her to type in her mobile phone number on the debit card reader at checkout. If she chooses the e-receipt option and opts in, the e-receipt will be delivered by free text message after the transaction is complete.*

---

[138] *http://www.bbc.co.uk/newsbeat/21499552*

[From E-mail Marketing - Wal-Mart will turn the electronic receipt into a sales tool - Internet Retailer]

This seems a little clunky, a little interim, to me but there are other implementations of electronic receipts emerging. Square's new "Feedback" product will extend electronic receipt capabilities to smaller merchants and go further to allow consumers to give instant input after paying for something using Square but inviting feedback on the delivery of an electronic receipt, and will give those kinds of small businesses a way to interact more intimately with customers.

"What if we saw it as a communication channel," he asked. "What if we saw it as a publishing medium, what if we saw it as a connection, and a reminder, and a potential for more of those experiences?"

[From Jack Dorsey Is Planning to Reinvent the Humble Receipt | TIME.com]

So, yes, e-receipts are inevitable. But I wonder about the managed kind of e-receipt. If I was a retailer, I'd want to convert to e-receipts in my own wallet, not in someone else's. If I were Waitrose, I'd want my app to do this, of course, because if they allow third-parties to manage the receipts for me, then that means those third-parties will get access to the level 3 POS data (the detailed line item data) and I'm sure they won't want that to happen. This what some of the players are working on.

The idea is to know far more than Clubcard can about consumers because – with all the necessary consents – this is a system that can span the high street and online retail, effortlessly connecting the dots.

[From Receipts: the digital future - Telegraph]

The future narrative for the retail app with payments and receipts will, surely, be that I amble into Waitrose, my Waitrose app opens automatically because of BLE and displays my shopping list and notes, I get a coffee (and wander around self-scanning my groceries. When I've finished, I tap out using NFC and the Waitrose app (which has used the Partnership Services API to pull down an HCE token for my John Lewis MasterCard) pays via the standard contactless terminal and checks me out, at which point the till knows that as I'm using the Waitrose app I don't want a stupid paper receipt and just sends the receipt back via NFC (or over the air using the interweb tubes) into the Waitrose app. Using the app and the "small data" tools provided by Waitrose I can then search, print, export or do whatever else I want to with my receipts - I'm not smart enough to imagine what else I actually might want to do with the receipts but I'm sure innovative persons will find some amazing things to do with them.

One final point about receipts. They need to be secure. You might think that they don't need the same degree of security as payments, but I think you're wrong. It's time to bring digital signatures to bear on them to ensure that when you pull up an old receipt and present it for whatever purpose (returns, warranties, who knows what) the system can depend on its integrity.

> To begin to comprehend China's vast underground economy, one need only visit this city's major transportation depots and watch as peddlers openly hawk fake receipts.

> A scalper mumbles, "Fapiao, fapiao," or receipts, at the Shanghai Railway Station. The trade in receipts is more or less open.

> "Receipts! Receipts!" calls out a woman in her 30s to passers-by as her two children play near the city's south train station. "We sell all types of receipts."

> Buyers use them to evade taxes and defraud employers. And in a country rife with corruption, they are the grease for schemes to bribe officials and business partners.

> [From Coin of Realm in China Graft - Phony Receipts - NYTimes.com]

I was surprised on my first visit to Russia to see this same kind of business conducted openly in the subway system. When I went on to the Moscow subway for the first time, genuinely marvelling at the Stalinist splendour, I was given a couple of cards by a hawker as I passed by. I couldn't read them, so I asked one of our Russian hosts what they were, and he said that one was an advertisement for bogus receipts for travel and the other was an advertisement for bogus medical certificates. No-one seemed at all fazed by this..

Targetting decoupled debit (20th June)

There was a discussion about decoupled debit at a meeting I was in last week. The context is not germane to this post, but I referred someone to a super piece about Target's decoupled debit payment scheme that I'd seen in American Banker. It makes the central point that decoupled debit isn't only about the cost to the retailer but about the overall purchasing experience, including offers and rewards. If it was only about costs, the decoupled debit proposition would be under some pressure.

Store-branded debit cards were supposed to die after price caps on swipe fees took effect in 2011, since one of its major advantages was that it allowed retailers to avoid paying the hefty interchange fees that banks were charging. Those fees have fallen sharply over the last two years. Yet Minneapolis-based Target is showing that under the right circumstances, store-branded debit cards can still work for retailers.

[From Target Card Tests Future of Store-Branded Debit - American Banker Article][139]

Target are not the only people who think that this is true, although in an odd way they might be a key reason for stimulating the sector, and not because of their (considerable) success in persuading customers to use the Target Red product but because of their rather famous Target data breach. Remember, when the Target data began sloshing through the interweb tubes, a clear media message was that scheme cardholders were vulnerable, but Target's own cardholders were not.

National Payment Card Association's merchant-branded decoupled debit cards may be part of an industry-wide solution to preventing the next Target breach.

[From 2014 - Will The Target Breach Kill Branded Debit Cards? | PYMNTS.com][140]

I was not joking about the success of the product, by the way. It has been incredibly successful. It's something like 20% of the volume already in the early-adopting stores and set for further growth.

Consumers who have a Target debit card increase their spending by an average of 52%, according to a presentation the company made last year. In the second quarter of this year, sales on the debit cards surpassed sales on Target's credit cards for the first time, according to the company..

[From Target Card Tests Future of Store-Branded Debit - American Banker Article][141]

---

[139] *http://www.americanbanker.com/issues/178_168/target-card-tests-future-of-store-branded-debit-1061698-1.html*
[140] *http://www.pymnts.com/briefing-room/issuers/trends-in-debit-cards/2014/Will-The-Target-Breach-Kill-Branded-Debit-Cards*

Now, I suspect that this success has not gone unnoticed in a number of boardrooms, both in financial institutions and retailers.

> *some experts believe that store-branded debit cards will be part of the strategy employed by the Merchant Customer Exchange, or MCX, the fledgling consortium of retail chains that is looking to challenge the traditional electronic payments system.*
>
> *[From Target Card Tests Future of Store-Branded Debit - American Banker Article]*

The mention of MCX is interesting. Obviously there are all sorts of different models that MCX could adopt for its nascent payment scheme, but many observers focus on the direct-to-bank debit solution as the most likely nudge the mass market.

> *The MCX white knight, many think, is store-branded debit products, also known as decoupled debit.*
>
> *[From Commentary - MCX and the Giant Payments Networks: A Payments Fairy Tale | PYMNTS.com][142]*

I saw Dodd Roberts (from MCX) give an update on the scheme down in Melbourne recently, and he identified five drivers for MCX from the retail community.

Customer experience.

Consistency of solution.

Security.

Data.

Flexibility.

He also talked specifically about payments as critical success factor, and about how to address (as they see it) the "payments imbalance" and the "efficiencies for issuers and merchants", saying that MCX are going to deliver a mobile commerce app that will deliver a better shopping experience on a secure platform that safeguards "stakeholders' interests" and implements a "balanced, competitive payments ecosystem".

---

[141] *http://www.americanbanker.com/issues/178_168/target-card-tests-future-of-store-branded-debit-1061698-1.html?zkPrintable=true*
[142] *http://www.pymnts.com/commentary/mcx-and-the-giant-payments-networks-a-payments-fairy-tale/*

We continue to believe the funding sources for MCX's wallet are a combination of private-label credit, decoupled debit, and stored value (i.e., gift cards), rather than traditional (credit card) accounts... Merchants seem hopeful that the ACH system will move closer to real-time authorization, but acknowledged that scenario is likely a good 3-4 years away.

[From Retailers' Mobile Wallet Seen Delayed To 2015; Apple Boost? - Investors.com][143]

Now, the payment incumbents, such as Visa and MasterCard, are not stupid people -- in fact they are very clever people -- and they can read the newspapers just as well as me. There will be a new cost floor emerging as the merchants use mobile phones, apps and customer experience to drive consumers to choose ACH over alternatives ("Pay with your Tesco and get double points" is an easy proposition for them and the transaction is indistinguishable from a normal debit transaction to the average consumer). Therefore, the advantages of using scheme credit and debit will have to come from value-added services that deliver something to consumers and merchants alike, otherwise they will be nudged out of the loop.

Unless... Here's a thought experiment. What if the schemes decided to disrupt themselves? What if the schemes developed their own decoupled debit proposition that used "hard" tokenisation and the internet instead of plastic cards, chips and proprietary networks? I mean, I know Christensen is somewhat unfashionable this week, but he has a point doesn't he? They could call it super debit or turbo debit or something. Couldn't they?

No need for Oyster in London any more (9th September)

For the last few years, colleagues at Consult Hyperion have been working for Transport for London (TfL) on a really big, fun, interesting and challenging project to allow customers to use mass transit in London without having to have a transit card, using instead the contactless payment cards issued by banks. You might remember that back in 2011 we recorded a podcast with Shashi Verma and Will Judge at TfL when they talked about the ambition to move to "open loop" on one of the world's biggest transit networks. Well, open loop ticketing went live on the buses a couple of years ago and I wrote at the time that:

To make the simple tap-and-go work for millions of consumers taking millions of bus rides, reliably and securely, is very

---

[143] http://news.investors.com/technology/061114-704248-retailers-mcx-mobile-wallet-launch-faces-obstacles.htm

complicated. To hide all of the complexity from consumers and make the tap work in a few hundred milliseconds was a tall order. But they've done it, so well done TfL.

From *You wait ages for a contactless terminal then 8,500 turn up at once - Tomorrow's Transactions.*

This week, this tap-and-go convenience was extended across the whole TfL network. Wow. And I genuinely mean it. Wow.

Passengers on the tube and most of London transport can now travel using a contactless card... Passengers will not need tickets or Oyster smartcards on the tube, tram, DLR, London Overground and rail services that currently accept Oyster cards.

From *London tube introduces contactless payments | Money | theguardian.com.*

The mass market use of open loop on London's various modes of transport will be contactless debit cards. Don't forget to tap out, by the way, or you'll be charged the full fare. So long as you tap in and tap out, daily and weekly fare capping applies just as it does with Oyster so you have no need to worry about the cost of travelling across, around, over or under our fair capital.

And finally, as they say, it means a symbolic goodbye to my beloved Barclaycard Visa OnePulse, the best credit card the chaps in Northampton ever issued, and it's triple-interface goodness. So long old friend.

It's taken a lot of hard work to make something work this simply, this well and at this scale. A hearty well done to all.

We still haven't finished talking about mobile wallets (19th October)

For my day out of the office chairing part of the Digital and Mobile Wallet Summit in London, I thought I would be tough on the panelists and presenters and force them to say something new, but actually there was a lot of new experience to share, a lot of new thinking (and re-thinking) going on and plenty of talk about in the end.

I challenged the first panel of the day to come up with a working definition of what a digital wallet is, if only for the purposes of discussion during the day. After some interesting debate, they came up with a pretty good set of three bullets points that I think provide a framework for discussion:

Wallet as transaction **enabler**.

Wallet as communication **co-ordinator**.

Wallet as **collector** of experiences.

I think this is a rather useful way of structuring thinking and it maps to our ideas coming from a more technological perspective, so I think I'll try and use it for a conference presentation and see if it works. I thought the panel discussion, with its emphasis on the non-payment aspects of the wallet, reinforced my own prejudices about the central role of identity as a transaction enabler but also echoed the Euro Banking Association's recent opinion papers that I happened to have been reading on the train on the way to the event. There is one on Digital Identity called "From Check-out to Check-in" and one on Next Generation Retail Payments called "User Requirements for Next Generation Payment", and I found them both useful sources of ideas that I'll blog about in the near future.

The second panel, which was more focused on retail POS and the consumers, was looking at the kind of services that might be delivered using the wallet. One of the panel members was my old sparring partner Richard Brahams from the British Retail Consortium (BRC) and another was Alberto Perez Lafuente from Bank Inter (the first "HCE bank" out there), which made for an informative (and entertaining) exploration of a variety of perspectives, including a rather interesting diversion around the nature of future competition: are banks, retailers and everyone else going to end up playing bit parts in the movie of future commerce? Someone (I can't remember who) said that the "big five" of Facebook, Apple, Google, Amazon and PayPal would end up forming the "commerce layer" with the banks and retailers as their fulfilment mechanisms. I'm not sure I share that gloomy prognosis but it's certainly a point that there are some structural changes afoot and that stakeholders need to develop a strategy response to them.

One of those structure changes is, of course, the arrival of the digital and mobile wallet as a core component of future commerce. My feeling, to be honest, is that the wallet is unlikely to be an app or a single service but more of an infrastructure that the service providers will use, a position that I've held for some time.

During the rest of the day I also particularly enjoyed the case study on Lipa Na M-PESA from Kenya. Sitoyo Lopokoiyit, the head of the M-PESA strategy department at Safaricom, explained how the "pay by M-PESA" service was taking M-PESA to the point of sale. They already have 100,000 merchants signed up (making them Kenya's biggest "acquirer" as there are only 12,000 Visa/MC merchants) and hope to have 200,000 signed up by the end of the year. They charge 0.25% to 0.4% transaction fee, which is very competitive compared to cards. The merchants are using SIM-based mobile POS terminals to make secure payments. He also gave great case study of how Diageo have integrated the system into their ERP. Apparently, mobile already accounts for 10% of fuel purchases (where there are very thin margins) so it's gaining traction across retail sectors.

I also enjoyed Carol van Cleef's presentation on regulation. I ended up in a vigorous debate with Carol about the American AML regime, the FATF's 2013 recommendations on risk-based approaches to regulating low-value payments, the relative merits of European and US regulatory approaches, the lack of cost-benefit analysis around AML, the purpose of payment regulations and much, much more.

But the main takeaway from the day, and the point of this post, is the main takeaway from the first panel that several of the presenters (e.g., Mea Wallet from Norway) emphasised: It is a mistake to think of the digital wallet as being primarily -- or even mainly -- about payments. If I hadn't run out of time because I was arguing about the cost-benefit analysis around AML, I would have used my talk to relate the points made about identification, authentication and so on to the "3R" business model that we have been using with our clients to help them to develop their business strategies: Recognition, Reputation and Relationships. But more on this another day.

Chapter 10: Technology and Telecommunications

Apart from being some of the biggest businesses in the world (the telecommunications sector has two **trillion** dollars in annual revenues), telcommunications and media companies are creating the platform for the future of work and play. Choices that they make, about how these platforms work, define the downstream business models that can exist on them and thus we should be paying close attention to services, systems and schemes that they are building.

HCE for MNOs (27th February)

The GSMA were kind enough to ask me to give one of the breakfast briefings at the Mobile World Congress in Barcelona this year, so I gave a briefing on HCE. I thought this rather a brave choice, because the MNO's first reaction to HCE was one of horror, but I decided that as it's a really hot topic it would be great to tackle it head on and look for ways for MNOs to find new opportunities.

I was trying to encourage operators to see HCE (and to some extent BLE, which I spoke about in the Digital Commerce conference session in the afternoon) as opportunities and not threats. So I used my time to explore three points building on our framework for the five key wallet technologies for 2014 that I went into in more detail in that afternoon session..

First, the mobile wallet is being energised by a set of new technologies (discussed in more detail in "Retail and Transport") including proximity and vicinity **Interfaces**, identification and authentication and APIs. These interfaces enhance the user experience when using the mobile wallet, by providing new ways to link to the local environment. For example, a consumer can walk in to a store, the wallet will recognise the store using its vicinity (e.g., BLE) interfaces and up will pop in store information. The wallet will help the user navigate round the store, allowing them to tap on offers and initiate transactions using proximity (e.g., NFC) interfaces.

Secondly, when it comes to proximity interfaces, HCE is a wallet accelerator that supports business flows that are complementary to the MNO Secure Element (SE). It will accelerate the development of NFC services which will expand the number of services available to the consumer (eg, **Small Data**) and service providers (eg, **Tokenisation**), educate the consumer as to NFC's potential and eventually bring innovative applications to customer's handsets.

Finally, the core elements in the MNO SE proposition for payment, ticketing and other applications in wallets (including HCE) are the secure services that MNOs are perfectly positioned to provide through common **APIs** using industry-standard frameworks, supporting not only payment services but also identity. The MNO UICC provides an SE managed on the customers' behalf, ideally suited to provide secure services to these applications. Service Providers and MNOs can also use the UICC for storage or supplementary services such as **Customer Recognition**, thereby enhancing the user experience.

In the discussion that followed there were some comments about the extent to which these building blocks are already in place. I tended to the optimistic: I think the operators have many of these blocks already, the GSMA are co-ordinating them through their digital commerce initiatives and there seem to be commercial imperatives for moving forward. This week has in fact already seen a key announcement in just this space.

> *The Mobile Connect service will simplify consumers' lives, offering a single, trusted, mobile phone number-based authentication solution that fully respects their online privacy.*
>
> *[From leading mobile operators unveil mobile connect initiative to provide consistent and interoperable approach to managing digital id]*[144]

Look, we all understand that HCE bypasses the SE. But that's a good thing: it simplifies and enables the deployment of transactional applications through mobile phones. That does not mean that the operators are totally bypassed if they get their acts together. The operators had, in retrospect unwisely, decided to found their NFC framework on the SE. HCE doesn't mean the SE is toast: it means that operators should use the SE for something that banks and other services providers <u>want</u> to use, and identity may well be it.

The afternoon session that I spoke at was in the Digital Commerce stream. I presented on the five technologies that will change the wallet in 2014 and then took part in an interesting panel discussion with my fellow presenters from Weve, Telecom Italia, BCC Card (Korea), Etisalat and SITA to discuss different aspects of the mobile's role in digital commerce.

At the end of the day, I feel that, overall, my prejudices were reinforced. I'm not sure if MNOs should be providing wallets, but there seems to be an opportunity for them to provide wallet infrastructure for other people to use to build wallets. The sky hasn't fallen in - there is a role for the SE if

---

[144] *http://www.gsma.com/newsroom/leading-mobile-operators-unveil-mobile-connect-initiative/*

the telcos decide to make strategic choices around infrastructure and focus on interoperable identification and authentication..

Tokenisation takes time (8th April)

One of the water cooler topics, as I believe they are called, at the excellent BAI Payments Connect in Las Vegas was tokenisation, which seems to have become bound up with the issue of Host Card Emulation (HCE) and the revitalisation of Near-Field Communication (NFC). The reason they have become bound up (when, logically, the two are quite separate: you can have HCE without tokenisation and you can have tokenisation with HCE) is because the two of them together form an attractive proposition for the payment schemes. Tom Noyes puts it bluntly.

> *Visa/MA prefer HCE to NFC hands down. It allows them to own the tokenization of cards in mobile. HCE actually ALIGNS to bank and network (V/MA) objectives: keep intelligence in network and control with issuers. The Networks ARE the TSMs.*
>
> *[From HCE - Now the PREFERRED contactless approach | Starpoint Blog - Finventures][145]*

This is all true. It does not, however, necessarily mean that mobile network operators (MNOs) are out of the loop. As I said at Mobile World Congress (MWC), just because the payment application isn't in the Secure Element (SE) that doesn't mean that the MNOs could not have other applications in the SE that third parties such as banks would want to use because they provide added value. An obvious example might be standardised FIDO clients that could use the low-level authentication capabilities built in to handsets (such as fingerprint readers) but shield service providers from the complexities.

Putting HCE to one side, though, I wanted to make a point about the complexity of tokenisation. It is hard. It is worth doing, absolutely. But it is complicated, and it is going to take some time to work it out. A couple of the banks I was chatting to in Vegas were asking why, so I thought I'd make a couple of general points to help organisations who are sketching out their strategy in this space now that the first draft of the specifications has been released (do yourself a favour and just skip to section 9.2 and go through the use cases!).

Many of the stakeholders want tokens to be the platform for adding value as well as reducing costs. The enhanced "customer recognition" capabilities of a mobile device certainly,a means to deliver reduced costs

---

[145] *http://blog.starpointllp.com/blog/?p=3638*

for the merchants, but, for added-value, tokens will have to provide something more than simple payment data along the lines of the alias PAN.This means the eventual standards will necessarily be more complex.

The new standard would include new data fields for richer transactional information to help improve fraud detection and expedite approval; consistent methods to identify and verify a user before issuing a token, and a common standard to simplify contactless and online transactions for merchants.

[From Visa, MasterCard, Amex mobile payments power play faces significant challenges - Mobile Commerce Daily - Payments][146]

Of course, we would all like these facilities at the in-store POS as well, which must be one of the things that EMVCo (who have been handed the responsibility of co-ordinating the standard) are thinking about. It would be jolly helpful all round if EMV 2.0 or son-of-EMV provided a route to convergence so that the distinction between "card present" and "card not present" fades away.

"Payment tokens also include enhanced data fields to provide richer information about the transaction" said Christina Hulka, EMVCo Board of Managers Chair

[From Tokenization standard in the works - ABA Banking Journal][147]

These enhanced data fields might well include data coming back from the merchant (e.g., electronic receipts) as well as additional data going to the merchant (e.g., coupons) and you can see that this degree of integration could deliver a very appealing proposition for merchants and consumers. So, as I said, complicated but worthwhile.

(There's a further complexity with tokens. The tokens cannot be independent from the associated account. There are many reasons for wanting to link together tokenised transactions, so it is not just a matter of generating tokens and leaving it at that. Suppose I buy something with token and then I want to take it back to return it? How can the retailer know whether my card was actually linked to the token they saw? For this reason, token transactions need to carry some incomplete information

---

[146] *http://www.mobilecommercedaily.com/visa-mastercard-amex-mobile-payments-power-play-faces-significant-challenges*
[147] *http://www.ababj.com/component/k2/item/4391-tokenization-standard-in-the-works*

about the associated card. In the current specification this is the last four digits of the PAN).

Managing all of this is going to be complicated and it has to work right every time at population scale. We're working hard with our clients to help them to develop the most appropriate strategies to their needs and then set out practical tactics to execute them, but it's going to take time to get everything in place and on a roadmap going forwards..

Contactless and crime (6th June)

Although we don't focus on it -- by and large because it works and has become business as usual -- I think that contactless payment technology is fun. I had an enjoyable couple of days trying out my usual panoply of cards, phones, watches and stickers when I was last in Canada and I have to report that the situation was all systems go (except for one of my UK MasterCards that was inexplicably declined) whereas in the US it remains mixed. Meanwhile, it's going gangbusters down under, as I discovered on my last trip to Australia. I paid with cards everywhere, and almost everywhere I paid I paid with contactless. Like in this taxi, for example.

Unfortunately, the Aussie rozzers are less enthusiastic than I am about the amazing technology, the rapidly-evolving Australian retail payment environment, innovation at point of sale and quick and easy transactions for consumers. They claim, in fact, that there is wave, plague and apocalypse of crime that can be directly attributed to the new technology.

> *"We're seeing many, many theft of motor cars, handbags and burglaries where people are looking for these cards, are getting hold of them and within hours of getting them, they're going into stores and using them.*

> *[From Tap-and-go credit cards contributing to increase in crime stats, Victoria Police says - ABC News (Australian Broadcasting Corporation)]*

This is, if true, rather interesting. I say "if true", of course, because I have been unable to uncover any statistics that back up the Victoria police claim. Nor, it seems, have any of their fellow law enforcement agencies.

> *Police around the country have differing views on the effect the cards are having on burglaries. The NSW Police said it had "not seen a spike in credit card related fraud since the advent of contactless payment technology".*

> *[From Banks stare down police over tap-and-go]*

Still, this tidal wave of contactless crime must surely have shown up in the bank fraud statistics.

> *One of the major banks said on Thursday it had 30 per cent more -contactless cards in the market compared with a year ago but card fraud was flat.*

> *[From Banks stare down police over tap-and-go][148]*

Oh well. Let's just assume for sake of argument that there is a crime wave, plague and apocalypse but only in Victoria and only amongst issuers who do no collect or report card fraud statistics. That still sounds like a bank problem to me, since issuers will bear the losses. If a mugger demands my contactless card then I will give it to him. I couldn't care less since it's not my problem: the UK banks have an unequivocal guarantee to refund unauthorised transitions. Nevertheless, the Melbourne heat seem most upset about contactless in general and especially miffed that they were not one of the stakeholders consulted in the banks' roll-out.

> *he said police were not consulted before tap-and-go credit cards were introduced and that he regretted their introduction... "They are chewing up an enormous amount of police resources.*

> *[From Tap-and-go credit cards contributing to increase in crime stats, Victoria Police says - ABC News (Australian Broadcasting Corporation)]*

The crime wave, by the way, does not seem to have affected public confidence, since contactless use continues to soar. It is at very high levels in Australia already, with more than two-thirds of supermarket transactions already tap and go. Use amongst police chiefs, so far as the statistics presented in the article would indicate, seems particularly high.

> *Mr Lay did admit he used a tap-and-go card all the time.*

> *[From Tap-and-go credit cards contributing to increase in crime stats, Victoria Police says - ABC News (Australian Broadcasting Corporation)][149]*

---

[148]

http://www.afr.com/p/business/financial_services/banks_stare_down_police_over_tap_1DUAxI3Ig3NeSN4f7aFsKM

[149] http://www.abc.net.au/news/2014-05-28/crime-rises-by-five-percent-according-to-latest-victoria-police/5483190

Aha. I should point out, by the way, that the Victorian peelers objections to contactless go back some time. They've always been uncomfortable with contactless.

Police want to ban banks' tap and go technology after vowing to take on big business over sloppy work practices. The force said it is sick of "mopping up" for "totally slack" initiatives that it states encourage crime.

[From Police want ban on tap and go technology, saying sloppy practices can promote crime | Herald Sun][150]

We have to address real issues, of course, but the fact is that public perception around contactless is not always rational. That Australian story was widely reported in the British press, fuelling public concerns (I have made a fascinating podcast with Karen Williams from Spectrum Insight on this topic). The British press have, it seems to me, always been rather keen on these scare stories. See this hilarious comment on a Daily Mail story about contactless.

It is well known that in America, thieves carry tablets and electronic readers in bags, walk around railway stations and shopping malls and scoop up all data automatically from these cards.

[From Customers charged twice for items because contactless cards were activated from their pockets | Mail Online][151]

Really? "Well-known"? If anyone can point to me a single reputable report of this ever happening, I would be grateful as I would like to link to it and continue the investigation. Far from being "well-known" I frankly doubt that it has ever happened at all. If you jammed an electronic reader up against my arse on the Tube, and kept it there undetected long enough to scan my card (I only have one in London wallet - haven't you ever heard of card clash) then you would not get my name or the CVV for the card, so it's not much of master crime. You can't use the data to make a clone card and you can't use it to buy online. Neverthess, as the analysis of contactless sentiment I discussed earlier in the week show, just because something doesn't happen does not mean we can ignore it. If consumers believe it, then we must deal with it.

---

[150] *http://www.heraldsun.com.au/news/law-order/police-want-ban-on-tap-and-go-technology-saying-sloppy-practices-can-promote-crime/story-fni0fee2-1226769029022*
[151] *http://www.dailymail.co.uk/news/article-2327245/Customers-charged-twice-items-contactless-cards-activated-pockets.html*

I think we as an industry should probably be reacting to the "fear" area with some pretty clear messaging around how the technology works, how liabilities are distributed and the consumer protection that the combination provides.

[From <u>Contactless sentiment - Tomorrow's Transactions</u>][152]

The traditional way of educating the mass market in the UK about anything is to pester the BBC to include it as an EastEnders story line. I shall come back with some ideas soon, but since I haven't watched EastEnders for at least a decade, it may take some research to get a viable narrative.

HCE BLE EMV is a new way to pay (23rd July)

Most of you know Consult Hyperion as the consultancy of choice for organisations who want to exploit new technology for mass-market electronic transactions. But you may not know that for many years we have had our own full-time, in-house development team. We call this the Hyperlab, and it's a resource used by many of our clients to build prototypes and proof-of-concept demonstrators, to play around with new ideas and to try out new technologies to see if they might be useful in market deployment. As you might imagine, one group of technologies heavily used in Hyperlab at the moment are NFC, SE and HCE. But in recent months, there's been some experimentation going on with BLE. It's not relevant to say why or for which clients, but we have good reason for thinking that BLE will be taken up by many of our clients to support new customer experiences.

The question naturally arises, then, as to the relationship between the technologies in this group. Our clients are at the larger end of the scale, so when they invest in new technology (even if it is only for prototyping) they need to have a view of the roadmap with a path (or more typically, paths) to connect the technology push with the business pull in a sensible manner. To be specific, the question facing many of our clients is the choice of path connecting all of these technologies in the retail environment. Largely because of the dominant position of Apple in the mindspace, if not the marketspace, a lot of recent discussion has been around the pros and cons of NFC and BLE, which I think is in many ways an unproductive place to begin the conversation. And I am not alone.

NFC and Bluetooth Low Energy (BLE) will likely complement each other and coexist in the mobile ecosystem because their best

---

[152] *http://tomorrowstransactions.com/2014/06/contactless-sentiment/*

use cases differ, John Ekers, the CIO at Abnote said in his keynote presentation.

[American NFC Mobile Technology Adoption to be Spurred by the 'Big 3': HCE, BLE and EMV | RFID Technology News]

I think John's right about this and we have been advising our clients the same for a good while. In fact, as I wrote last year, there is no need to see any either/or in the combination. Some people like to tap. Some don't. Some people want to use a mobile wallet. Some people want to use a retailer app. Some people like to be recognised automatically. Some prefer to have control. So let them have their choices.

An HCE/NFC/BLE world seems rather attractive from a consumer experience perspective.

[From Why all the fuss about HCE? - Tomorrow's Transactions]

Now, since the nature of our business concerns transactions, we are particularly interested in the technologies around retail transactions. And since most of our clients have in recent memory spent an enormous amount of money migrating to EMV, it is naturally of interest to see how this transaction technology works with NFC and BLE. With this in mind, and in the context of a couple of projects we are working on, we thought it would be interesting to see if we could execute EMV transactions over the BLE vicinity interface. Obviously we know how to do this using the NFC proximity interface, and so does everybody else, but there are a couple of good reasons for trying it over BLE.

First of all, both Android phones and iPhones (and also other phones, and, for that matter, smart watches and the like) have BLE whereas they do not have NFC. This means the retailer app can deliver a common experience on both platforms. Since retailers want to use BLE to establish communication between location and customer, using it for payment as well is an obvious extension.

Secondly, a rich BLE interaction between the handsets and the point of sale or service can encompass coupons, loyalty, offers, information and all sorts of other valuable data as well as the payment data.

So we tried. And it worked. Stuart Fiske, our CTO, demonstrated it at UK Cards last week. The laptop in front of him was running the POS software and it has a BLE USB diongle connected. The power on the device was been dialled down to reduce the range (important for POS applications). Stuart was running a mobile wallet app on an Android phone. This app has real EMV credentials stored in it and used HCE to pretend to be an EMV card to the POS terminal.

The POS writes a payment request to the BLE dongle. This request contains the EMV data fields that are needed to effect a transaction with a standard EMV card. The request is broadcast and picked up by the mobile wallet app. The app takes the data fields and feeds them to the HCE app, where the relevant EMV jiggery-pokery goes on and a bunch of data fields are generated. These are fed back to the POS terminal, where the EMV data elements are stripped out and passed on to the acquiring system. Note that the acquiring system has no idea that these data elements came from HCE via BLE: all it sees are the same EMV data fields that it would see in a normal interaction with a standard EMV terminal.

The transaction is approved, and the customer has paid, securely, while standing near a POS terminal or POS person or mPOS or vending machine or... You get the point. It's cool. And here's the fun part: here's the same app running on an iPhone. Yes, that's right. HCE on an iPhone, but using BLE instead of NFC to pay.

Just as a further point, you can see how this might work with tokenisation. The iPhone/Android bank/retailer/whoever app would periodically contact the relevant token vault to pre-fetch tokens valid for an hour or a day or a particular merchant. Then, when the customer walks into the branch/shop/wherever, the app opens up and displays coupons, loyalty points, shopping lists and so forth. The customer gets what they want, it gets rung up either at a conventional POS or on a handheld POS. Then the consumer executes an EMV payment either by tapping with an NFC phone or confirming on a BLE phone. Either way, it's a secure transaction that uses the standard EMV infrastructure to deliver a terrific payment experience in the context of a terrific shopping experience.

Our Hyperlab guys rock.

Never mind the last mile, what about the last inch (25th June)

Here's a quick payment quiz. Have a guess before you click on the link! Which of the approximately 10,000 new payment solutions that are under development right now works this way:

> The system generates a unique QR code that allows a payment to be made, but no customer information or shopping data is passed onto the merchant, and all transaction receipts are kept on the app.

[From Samsung Favors QR Over NFC | PYMNTS.com][153]

---

[153] http://www.pymnts.com/news/2014/samsung-favors-qr-over-nfc/

The Tomorrow's Transactions Reader 2015

Well, if you guessed "all of them" you're nearly right, but actually it's a new payment system from Samsung (who make the S5, amongst other contactless-capable handsets) in Australia (which has a couple of hundred thousand contactless payment terminals in place and the highest retail use of contactless in the world). Why are they doing this? It's not because QR codes are the best solution — they aren't — but because better alternatives (NFC and Bluetooth Low Energy) have not been available. But they are now, which makes the Samsung launch rather surprising to me.

I used to think that I was abnormal because I can't be bothered to scan QR codes, but it turns out that I'm actually quite mainstream.

In all of the time I've had a phone with a camera and an application for reading QR codes, which is quite a long time, I've probably used the functionality two, or at a maximum three, times. I wondered if this might be because I am old or because I am lazy or because I am insufficiently inquisitive, but actually it's because I am normal.

[From A quick response to the problem - Tomorrow's Transactions][154]

Whereas I can't be bothered to run a QR application and scan a code, I'm quite prepared to just tap on something or have something auto-open on my iPhone for me to confirm. Having been involved in quite a few NFC trials, pilots and tests I'm confident in saying that most people are the same. Consumers were perfectly happy to tap to get what they wanted and, as far as I can recall, actually rather liked it. It was the supply chain that didn't work.

In other words, NFC is great but not yet relevant. This, to be honest, seem like a pretty reasonable assessment of the current situation and contains both good and bad news. The bad news is that the money that the payments industry is spending on NFC will have a much longer payback time than had been hoped. The good news is that we (consumers) end up with something that is simple and quick and secure.

[From Tomorrow's Transactions][155]

So, as has been known for some time, this is generally true. When people are given the option of tapping, for example, over scanning then they greatly prefer it. The barrier to NFC in the mass market was never the consumer.

---

[154] *http://tomorrowstransactions.com/2012/02/a-quick-response-to-the-problem/*
[155] *http://tomorrowstransactions.com/page/2/?s=QR+NFC*

*An analysis conducted by NFC specialist Connecthings has found
that NFC phone users account for a disproportionate percentage
of interactions with its NFC- and QR code-based marketing and
information services platform*

*[From Firm finds NFC users interact more than QR code users •
NFC World+][156]*

For these and other reasons (to do with security), I've always seen QR
codes as an interim solution, something that will let people try out ideas
(e.g., Bitcoin wallets) while we wait for something better to come along,
but never the mass-market strange attractor for next-generation payments,
no matter how much I like LevelUp. And it turns out that the man who
invented QR codes agrees.

*QR codes have seen a range of improvements through its 20
years, but Hara mentions that he believes that NFC and better
image recognition will supplant the QR codes' role.*

*[From QR Codes Will Be Gone in Ten Years Says Its Inventor
»][157]*

For those already in the QR code space this isn't particularly bad news in
my opinion. Or, at least it isn't for those who used the right consultants to
help them to architect their solutions in the first place... The QR code is
simply the "last millimetre" connection between the merchant and the
consumer. Almost all of the systems that people have built are not to do
with this: so if the last millimetre replaces the QR code with the more
convenient NFC/BLE combination, then their solution will be even better
and more convenient than it was before. We will certainly be advising our
clients to structure their solutions so that that swapping out the last
millimetre can be painless and cost-effective.

The Phoney War is over (28th October)

As has been remarked more than once, and in many contexts, if your
wallet gets stolen then it's your driving licence, social security card and
Portugese fishing licence that are the problem, not your money. Remember
your Shakespeare! "He who steals my purse steals trash" (Othello: Act 3,
Scene 3). It's your identity that is the valuable thing in your wallet, the
thing you should leave locked up in the hotel room safe instead of being

---

[156] *http://www.nfcworld.com/2012/02/14/313202/firm-finds-nfc-users-interact-
more-than-qr-code-users/*
[157] *http://paymentweek.com/2014-6-20-qr-codes-will-gone-ten-years-says-
inventor-4937/*

The Tomorrow's Transactions Reader 2015

forced carry it around with you in case you want to buy something - as I am required to do in the US, where you often still have to sign your name when you use a payment card in a shop.

If I'm right, then my identity should only be entrusted to organisations who understand security and privacy and, most importantly, actually know who I am.

Britain's high street banks believe their future role will be as repositories of more than just money: they want to be the safe place where customers store their digital identities.

[From Banks want to keep your digital ID in their vaults - FT.com][158]

It's natural to think of banks in this role and, despite the fact that I can't use my bank identity to log in to anything other than my bank at the moment, reasonable to imagine that their plans for forming a trusted identity layer to underpin the new economy are well advanced.

Banks are well positioned as is explained in a recent white paper (link) of the European Banking Association (EBA).

[From Digital Identity: how banks can position themselves in their customer's online lives | Innopay][159]

It is also natural for people (e.g., journalists) to see the identity issue in terms of payments, because payments are where we most urgently need a solution. The myriad data breaches mean that efforts are focused on online purchases and the use of the decades-old PAN-centric card infrastructure in an environment it was never designed for.

Some suggest that digital identity verification by banks could ultimately end the need to type in a credit-card number on an ecommerce website

[From Banks want to keep your digital ID in their vaults - FT.com][160]

The FT are right. Identity could be a huge play for banks. Mind you, some others (uncharitable persons, of which I am not one) also suggest that

---

[158] http://www.ft.com/cms/s/0/9c1e4b06-328b-11e4-93c6-00144feabdc0.html#axzz3CX2odR2P
[159] https://www.innopay.com/content/digital-identity-how-banks-can-position-themselves-their-customer-s-online-lives
[160] http://www.ft.com/cms/s/0/9c1e4b06-328b-11e4-93c6-00144feabdc0.html#axzz3CX2odR2P

banks will prat about and muck this all up and hand digital identity verification to Apple, Facebook, Google, Amazon and Microsoft on a plate. Many years ago, I thought this wouldn't happen because I thought that the banks would come to some arrangement with the mobile operators since (at the time) the mobile operators were the only providers of tamper-resistant hardware with a communications link: the SIM.

The Norwegian implementation follows my favourite SimID model: the service providers use virtual IDs (public key certificates), the mobile operator provides the digital identity (the key pair) and the bank binds the digital identity to the real person.

[From Norwegians would - Tomorrow's Transactions][161]

I rather liked the model that this suggested. Go to log on somewhere and have a message pop up on my phone, enter a local passcode on the phone, find myself logged in on the web. I was a strong advocate of a pseudonymous option around this, so that service providers would know that you have been authenticated, but not who you were (the bank could provide a unique and cryptographically-unlinkable token to each service provider).

Now that my bank has an app on my mobile phone, you might imagine that they could perform this role (for a small fee) not only for payments but for more general cases. For example, suppose I need to log on to a gambling web site and prove that I am over 18? That's exactly where this sort of bank recognition could work. I give the gambling web site my mobile phone number, they send it to a [currently nonexistent] bank directory service and moments later my mobile banking app pops up on my phone and asks me to log in.

In recent years, though, we don't seem to have seen much progress in this field and now that Apple (and, inevitably, Google) have decided to bypass the operator SIM and use their own tamper-resistant hardware in the handset, surely the banks' potential as key, trusted identity players is under threat. Maybe it's time for them to take the whole ID thing seriously and start coming up with new ideas.

This article asks if there is a specifically British problem with identity fraud, what with identity fraud being something like half of all fraud in the UK. Actually, I don't think there is, but read on...

A recent victim had a fraudulent bank account opened in her name using details obtained from a photo of herself holding her

---

[161] *http://tomorrowstransactions.com/2006/12/norwegians_woul/*

driving licence – originally posted (doubtless in celebratory spirit) on Instagram.

[From [Invasion of the scammers: why is Britain so vulnerable? | News | The Week UK][162]

Sounds like the rigorous KYC, AML and ATF (customer due diligence, or CDD) procedures being enforced by banks are really working, doesn't it? No wonder AML costs for UK banks were up by more than a half last year. But it isn't a UK problem. It's global, there's no doubt about it.

Police say the male thief and his accomplices went right across the parking lot to Chase Bank, where they got a $10,000 cash advance using Martha's credit card and license. The next day, they got a moving violation on the freeway and showed police Martha's license. When they failed to show up in court, the DMV suspended Martha's license.

[From [Revealed: Tricks Thieves Use to Steal From You in Supermarket | NBC Southern California][163]

So the gazillions spent on CDD can't stop a male thief from getting cash from a bank using a female victim's driving licence and credit card. Amazing. You would think that there was a point to banks demanding to see your driving licence (not only banks - I was asked for photo ID when buying a coffee in Starbucks), but there really isn't, because they have no way of verifying it. They just photocopy it and put it on file so they can tick the box and prove they have complied with CDD. They haven't really ID'd you.

In fact, the issue of ID, and which ID you might have to show in order to effect any particular transactions is particularly fascinating to me. I anticipate a balkanisation, a move away from a universal ID to ID's that are specific to communities, to transaction types and to services. Speaking at the Tomorrow's Transactions Forum a couple of years ago, "Long Finance" author Gill Ringland said that she thought that in the coming era of the C50 there would be a new asset class around demographics, because the ability to live in particular cities would be very valuable: my Woking ID might be more valuable than my British Passport. In fact it already is in one respect: a British passport doesn't count as ID at Woking library

---

[162] *http://www.theweek.co.uk/prosper/58387/invasion-scammers-why-britain-so-vulnerable*
[163] *http://www.nbclosangeles.com/investigations/series/shopping-for-your-money/Revealed-Tricks-Thieves-Use-to-Steal-From-You-in-Supermarket-258060931.html?_osource=SocialFlowFB_LABrand*

because it doesn't show that you live in Woking so I had to come home to get other ID to go back and get a library card.

But back to identities. In countries without identity cards, such as the UK and the US, I suppose it is reasonable to expect that people can open bank accounts using photographs taken from random strangers' Instagram streams. But in countries with an identity card, surely it is very different. Oh, wait...

> *Fake cards are commonly used to hide ill-gotten property and gains from banks, purchase multiple sets of property in cities where owning more than one home is illegal and let citizens enjoy increased health care and social benefits at school and work*
>
> *[From Shanxi police chief has 8 false identities, 7 fake names | ChinaHush]*[164]

Just as the people of South Korea have discovered, having a centralised state-mandated universal identity doesn't fix the problem. Identity is broken, people. Broken.

So. Where next? Who might provide the useful, practical, workable, secure, trusted, specific identities that are specific to communities, transactions and services? Well, one obvious candidate class is banks. The Euro Banking Association's Working Group on Electronic Alternative Payments published an opinion paper on Digital Identity back in May. It was called "From check-out to check-in" and it is rather good. It specifically calls for:

The unbundling of the banks' valuable authentication services from payments. (This is what we used to call NPA, or "non-payment authentication" when we were doing studies on it for our clients about a decade ago.)

Enabling controlled (by customers) availability of valuable information, somewhat along the lines of the SWIFT "Digital Asset Grid" (DAG).

Setting up and positioning digital identity services towards the market, which is where there is a focus of interest amongst some of our clients right now.

Now, as anyone with even the most casual acquaintance with Consult Hyperion's thought leadership activities in the field for the last decade will

---

[164] *http://www.chinahush.com/2014/05/01/shanxi-police-chief-has-8-false-identities-7-fake-names/*

attest, this is hardly a new idea. We have been consistently advising our clients in this direction for some considerable time.

Adrian's comment about banks getting into the digital identity business hits the nail on the head from my perspective. Dave Birch talks about this all the time and he is right.

[From The Financial Services Club's Blog: Why can't banks behave more like IT companies?][165]

So it's interesting to ask: why now? Why are banks suddenly interested in the world of digital identity again? Not only at the European level. In the UK, for example, Barclays' decision to join OIX (a not-for-profit trade association in this space) alongside Google, Experian, the Cabinet Office and others served to flag up the potential for banks to be big, big players in the future environment.

Forget current accounts and savings bonds. Britain's high street banks believe their future role will be as repositories of more than just money: they want to be the safe place where customers store their digital identities.

[From Banks want to keep your digital ID in their vaults - FT.com][166]

I agree with this vision, as it happens. I think the idea of some sort of "Financial Services Passport" is a good one, and a good place to start (in fact in my role as Chair of the techUK Payments Group I've been chairing some discussions about precisely this idea) but I would expect this to be only one of the range of identities that banks could offer.

Trying to develop a roadmap in this area is, however, not straightforward. A couple of years ago, I guess we would all have agreed that "top down" identity — whether from banks or government — was the inevitable way forward. But now we have social networks, mobile phones and Bitcoin. Yes, Bitcoin. In his much-linked talk at Le Web, the well-known venture capitalist Fred Wilson said that "we have allowed Google and Facebook to become our de facto identity services" and he predicted that a "Bitcoin-like" identity protocol will arise in the future. Interesting. In other words, for Bitcoin as for everything else, identity is the new money. There's so much happening it's hard to know where to begin to formulate business strategy.

---

[165] *http://thefinanser.co.uk/fsclub/2014/10/why-cant-banks-behave-more-like-it-companies.html*
[166] *http://www.ft.com/intl/cms/s/0/9c1e4b06-328b-11e4-93c6-00144feabdc0.html#axzz3GTpv94mc*

Chapter 11: Public Services and NGOs

Digital identity, digital money and digital networks have the long-recognised potential to transform the delivery of public services as much as they have the ability to revolutionise commerce. The nature of public sector organizations, and often NGOs too, is that they can be slow to change their ways: even if they adopt new technology, their governance, ethos and budgets can conspire to make them conservative in their use of it. Nevertheless, the way in which they adopt these technologies will have a profound impact on the lives of a great many people around the world..

Electronic voting, electronic ID, electronic entitlement (20th January)

At Consult Hyperion, we are interested in electronic voting for three main reasons:

- We are thought leaders in the digital identity space and electronic voting is a key "stress" application for digital identity;

- We advise public sector clients on national identity and identity-related schemes (eg, the Irish Government's Public Services Entitlement Card);

- While people think about electronic voting in national and other political elections, there are a great many other applications of interest to our clients. A good example is the use of electronic voting for corporate purposes to replace postal voting at shareholder meetings, where the techniques developed for political elections could be used to reduce costs.

The practical deployment of, and experiences learned from the use of, new electronic voting systems are invaluable input into the wider question of identity infrastructure for a modern society, which is why we were delighted to be able to sponsor the 4th International Conference on e-Voting and Identity at the University of Surrey last year. This turned out to be an excellent event and we learned a lot about the different approaches to the problem, constraints, potential solutions and so on. As it happens, there are a great many practical problems around voting, and the solutions are complicated. But there are real social needs that must be addressed, and one of them has just reappeared in the British media.

Voters should be required to show photo ID at polling stations in Great Britain to lessen the risk of fraud, the Electoral Commission has said.

The Tomorrow's Transactions Reader 2015

[From BBC Voters 'should be required to show photo ID at elections', says watchdog][167]

Personally, I'm in favour of voter IQ laws as well as voter ID laws, but there you go. While electoral fraud is not rampant in the UK, it is certainly not non-existent. The Electoral Commission in fact identified 16 out of the 400 local authority areas in the UK as being at risk, one of these being my own dear Woking[168], where we have a long and proud tradition of electoral fraud. The Electoral Commission highlighted the major problems that have been identified around postal voting (which I do not think should be allowed, but that's another issue). Foreign readers might be surprised to learn that when you go to vote in the UK you simply give your name and it is crossed off of a list of eligible voters, much as it was when the first Viscount Watkinson was returned as Woking's MP in 1950 when the constituency was created, or for that matter when Sir Talbot Buxomley was first elected MP for Dunny-on-the-Wold in the reign of George III. This arrangement is no longer immune from the suspicion of personation, so the Commission has recommended the use of photographic ID.

> *...people were concerned that a requirement for photographic identification would discriminate against certain groups of electors, who would not necessarily have any form of photographic documentation, such as a passport or driving licence.*

[From Security Document World][169]

Similar issues are to the fore across the pond where the US voter ID situation is in a bit of a mess. If I understand the current situation properly, one of the problems with the just-introduced Voting Rights Amendment Act 2014, which is a response to the Supreme Court striking down part of the Voting Rights Act last year, is that there is potential for discrimination against people who are not able to obtain a "Voter ID" card. You can see their point. In other countries, this isn't a problem, because everyone has some form of ID card. But in the US which, like the UK, has no identity infrastructure, the "systems" developed for other purposes will have to be sub-optimally commandeered. This is the sort of thing that is going to be proposed in, to pick a random example, Nevada.

---

[167] http://www.bbc.co.uk/news/uk-politics-25641801
[168] http://www.theguardian.com/uk/2005/mar/28/politics.election2005
[169]
http://www.securitydocumentworld.com/public/news_all.cfm?&m1=e_0&m2=e_0 &m3=e_0&m4=e_0&subItemID=3384

The new voting system also would link with Department of Motorized Vehicle's license database, allowing poll workers to visually verify the identity of the person attempting to vote.

[From Nevada secretary of state gets mixed reaction to voter verification proposal - Las Vegas Sun News][170]

Since the British government recently announced that it was going to put driving licence details online anyway, then I imagine there would be some pressure to use this database, despite its being known to be notoriously inaccurate. But what else do British subjects have to hand with a photograph on it, if not a passport or driving licence? My son could use his student ID card, I suppose (although I am rather against allowing students to vote, on principle), although I've no idea how it might be verified on the day. Perhaps they could ask us to sign to vote and compare the signature against... what?

On a recent expedition to New York I was asked for photo ID as condition of entrance to a well-known landmark. I produced the (expired) building pass for our Madison Avenue office and was waved through. Which illustrates what is to me a central problem: if I am required to produce a photo ID at a polling station, it will do nothing to prevent fraud. The polling stations are manned by local volunteers doing their civic duty, not by expertly-trained anti-fraud personnel who are skilled in the inspection and detection of counterfeit identity documents. If I show up to vote and present a driving licence, a Portugese fishing licence or an England football club supporter's card, the polling station staff will have no means to verify it. As it happens, some UK pressure groups are against photo ID in principle anyway, because it discriminates against people who don't have a photo ID. Consequently,

the idea of voters being requested to provide a non-photographic form of identification at the polling station was welcomed in principle by both the public and electoral administrators.

[From Security Document World][171]

This seems utterly stupid to me but it is certainly in the great British tradition of pointless activity! It follows the tried and tested political theory of "something must be done, this is something, therefore it must be done". So the Mother of Parliaments will rest on a franchise that is

---

[170] *http://www.lasvegassun.com/news/2013/jan/11/nevada-secretary-state-gets-mixed-reaction-voter-v/*
[171]

http://www.securitydocumentworld.com/public/news_all.cfm?&m1=e_0&m2=e_0&m3=e_0&m4=e_0&subItemID=3384

protected by photocopies of gas bills, since as we all know, electoral terrorists dedicated to subverting democracy will be unable to forge those. Not that I can produce one anyway, because my gas bill is electronic.

Compared to this, the TSA's decision to accept Facebook profiles as valid identity for boarding flights in the US seems sound. On balance, I judge it to be far harder to forge a plausible Facebook profile than a plausible gas bill, so if I turn up at the polling station and log in to the Facebook profile for David Birch (if there is a Facebook profile for a David Birch, incidentally, I can assure you it isn't me) then they may as well let me vote.

The USA's Transport Security Administration is accepting sight of a traveller's Facebook profile as a form of ID, it has emerged.

[From Facebook profile accepted as ID at airport security][172]

One can imagine that this approach might itself still be further secured by the addition of photo ID. There's an app for that…

An upcoming app for Android, iOS, and Google Glass called NameTag will allow you to photograph strangers and find out who they are -- complete with social networking and online dating profiles.

[From Facial recognition app matches strangers to online profiles | Crave - CNET][173]

So all we need to do is equip the polling clerks with Google Glass and job done? I don't think so. I think we should think about what infrastructure is needed here and then work out the best to way implement it. There are a great many circumstances in which I would certainly imagine a Facebook profile to be a much better form of identification than a photocopy of my gas bill, but voting isn't one of them, especially if there are already concerns about fraud.

But Electoral Commission chairwoman Jenny Watson said most voters could use passports, driving licences or even public transport photocards to prove who they are at polling stations. Those without any of these documents could request a free elections ID card, she added.

---

[172] *http://www.thedrum.com/news/2014/01/03/facebook-profile-accepted-id-airport-security*
[173] *http://www.bbc.co.uk/news/uk-politics-25641801*

[From BBC <u>Voters 'should be required to show photo ID at</u> <u>elections', says watchdog</u>]

I am not making this up. Gas bills, Facebook profiles and railcards. That is where our democracy is in 2014. What a joke.

This is something.

The real solution is, of course, not using Railcards or football supporter's cards, or indeed special-purpose election ID cards, but a general-purpose National Entitlement Scheme (NES). Few readers will remember this, but some time before the UK government's last attempts to introduce a national identity card, there were consultations around a much better idea, which was a national entitlement card. As my colleague Neil McEvoy and I pointed out in Consult Hyperion's response to this consultation, the "card" is only one mechanism for storing and transporting entitlements and in the modern age there might be better ones, such as mobile phones for example, that can not only present credentials but also validate them.

It is time to revisit that proposal to try and get the British government out of its muddle about identity infrastructure. A future administration will certainly have to introduce something, not only because of the issue of voting fraud but due to continuing concerns about illegal immigration, health tourism, benefit fraud and so forth. Suppose that the vision for national identity (based on the concepts of social graph, mobile authentication, pseudonyms and so on) focused on the entitlement rather than on the transport mechanism or biographical details? Then, as a user of the scheme, I might have an entitlement (ie, a public key certificate) on my purpose-built national entitlement card (so that's some of the population taken care of), I might have a entitlement certificates on my bank card (so that's the overwhelming majority of the population taken care of) and I might have certificates in my mobile phone (so that's 99.9% of the population taken care of). Remember, these certificates would attest to my ability to do something: they would prove that I am entitled to do something (access the NHS, open my office door, buy things in Waitrose), not who I am. They are about entitlement, not identity as a proxy for entitlement. The government could give out free smart card readers (as they do in Spain) or leave it to the banks to distribute them.

In practice, I think the example set by a modern countries such as Turkey and Estonia are most attractive: I log in to the whatever with some pseudonym, the service provider sends a message to my mobile phone (over-the-air or via NFC or BLE in the future), the PKI in my SIM decodes the challenge and signs the response, and I'm connected. Securely and simply. And if other service providers want me to log on in the same way, they can issue their own certificates as well. There's a similar approach to this in Norway, except there the IDs are issued by the banks and used by the government and other private sector organisations. Imagine a national entitlement scheme that used this technology: it would be efficient and cost-effective, since it would use the phones that people already have to deliver services that they definitely want.

And, best of all, my phone would be able to check the entitlement presented by your phone, so none of us would need special equipment. I show up with my phone and claim that I am entitled to vote: my phone presents a meaningless but unique number, this is entered manually or automatically into the polling clerk's phone which flashes up my picture if I am entitled to vote or a red cross if I am not. I show up with my entitlement card and the polling clerk reads it using their NFC interface, and so on. Instead of postal votes, the polling clerk can go to the old folk's home and let them vote individually, certain that they are not being threatened or cajoled.

Should people be allowed to go one step further and simply log in to vote from home? For political elections, I think not. Voting must be in public in order to dispel any suspicion of coercion. Maybe it won't have to be a polling booth any more (you could have general elections that last a week during which people can vote at Post Offices or bank branches or whatever), but it has to be somewhere public.

Therefore it must be done.

It seems to me that a national plan to finally do something useful about identity might obtain "parasitic vitality" (to use one of my favourite ID phrases) from the specific issue of voter ID. In the UK and in the US, this might be a way to both improve security around the act of voting as well as a vector for deployment. Maybe electronic voting can be a focus to get the Cabinet Office's Identity Assurance (IDA) scheme a flagship and get the public and private sector working together to deliver an infrastructure that will be of benefit to all. I should mention in passing that we have been working with the Cabinet Office on one of their "Alpha Projects" in the North of England which, as it happened, included photo ID for authentication as one of the use cases.

Identity might work better bottom up (19th June)

Forum friend Kosta Peric from the Bill and Melinda Gates Foundation (BMGF) Financial Services for the Poor programme recently picked out four technologies as being of particular interest right now. He pointed us to:

bitcoin-inspired distributed systems,

> open APIs (application programming interface) as a new way to
> consume business services on the internet,
>
> crowd-sourced identity schemes, and
>
> open source hardware and applications.
>
> [From _Four Technologies That Will Revolutionize Financial_
> _Services | copernicc_]

I'm sure we'd all agree with his views on blockchain technologies and the
"Amazonisation" of financial services organisation through APIs (I don't
know enough about open-sourced hardware to comment) but I think his
point about crowd-sourced identity is especially interesting, as it points to
a shift in the way that identities are created, managed and used. And, since
I'm rather obsessed with identity right now (as our clients should be and,
in some cases, are too) I thought I'd take the time to explain why I agree
with him.

First, look at what the conventional, top-down notion of identity means. It
means someone (the government, generally speaking) must find some way
to assign an identity to everyone who needs one, record who those
identities have been assigned to, and check that when the identities are
presented they are genuine.

It is almost certain that the government is having difficulties establishing
who is a genuine citizen purely on the basis of identification papers
produced by the existing system. Some of the illegal immigrants caught in
the current security swoop have Kenyan ID cards and passports but their
details are not in the national database.

> It has been claimed that immigration and provincial
> administration officials at all levels have enriched themselves by
> selling these sensitive documents while compromising national
> security.
>
> [From _Kenyans to apply for digital identity cards, says Ruto_][174]

There are problems with this top down approach. Apart from being
expensive, it is also vulnerable. Once a false identity has been entered into
the system, it is no longer false (if you see what I mean). As a
consequence, obtaining such an identity becomes an essential precursor to
crime as well as legitimate use and therefore the identities are obtained by
all sorts of people who are not supposed to have them and the system is

---

[174] _http://www.midnimo.com/2014/04/15/kenyans-apply-digital-identity-cards-_
says-ruto/

subverted. Managing and protecting the database at the heart of this scheme is complicated and difficult. In a great many emerging markets, in particular, the national identity scheme is soon degraded: sometimes because of corruption, sometimes because of carelessness, sometimes because of errors in the concept and design. This is precisely what has happened with the Aadhar scheme in India.

What was supposed to be a unique identification number providing identification and access to a host of government benefits and services, 'Aadhaar' has almost unvaryingly been extended to anybody residing within Indian territories. Almost anyone, be it Indian or an illegal immigrant can get an Aadhaar Card made without any proof of identity. More importantly, they get a numbered identity.

[From Sting reveals Aadhaar documents forged for Nepal, Bangladesh citizens - IBNLive][175]

So how does the alternative, crowdsourced version of identity take us forward? Well, if national identity schemes don't provide "real" security then why bother with them? Save the money. At a basic level, crowdsourced identity means asking everyone who you are, rather than asking anyone (e.g., the government) who you are. Whereas we are used to the idea of identity as something that is granted to us by a third party, such as the government or a bank, the idea of an identity based on reputation that grows up through our networks and long-term relationships seems rather different.

Compare the two kinds of identity and their functionality in practice. Crowdsourced identity may seem a poor substitute for national identity at first glance, but it seems to me that Kosta is onto something here for two specific reasons that I have touched on before. The first is that this kind of reputational identity is actually **better** than conventional national identity because it is much harder to forge or counterfeit. A good friend of mine told me a story about an industry event he attended recently where he ran into a chap late at night when he was going back to his hotel. The guy was in the hotel lobby and recognised my friend as he had been a speaker at the event. The man explained that he had been tricked by a woman in a bar into following her back to hotel room where he had been drugged and robbed. He had no money and was too embarrassed to call his wife and asked if my friend might loan him some money so that he could get home and would report his wallet lost on the train or something. My friend had never met the man before but asked him his name and who he worked for and then looked him up on LinkedIn. Having established that not only did

---

[175] *http://ibnlive.in.com/news/aadhaar-officials-forge-papers-for-nepal-bangladesh-citizens-sting/459963-3.html*

the fellow have a full LinkedIn profile but was actually connected to my friend via several different people, my friend loaned him the money which was, of course, gratefully returned a couple of days later. Now imagine that the unfortunate chap had instead presented my friend with his Portuguese fishing licence: how would my friend evaluate that and assess the strangers plausibility from that official document?

The second reason is that these crowdsourced identities may well be far **cheaper** to establish and this is especially true, and especially valuable, in the developing world where official infrastructure may be unreliable at best and non-existent at worst. Here the particular combination of mobile phones and social networks is especially powerful, because mobile phones tend to deliver not only unique identity but transactional history to go with it and this can be linked through social networking in powerful ways. You might have listened to the podcast I recorded earlier this year with Shivani Siroya and and heard a very good example of this where the transactional histories from mobile payment accounts are slurped up by organisations who provide alternatives to conventional kind of credit reference agencies that we are used to in the developed world.

> *Shivani Siroya is currently the CEO and Founder of InVenture. InVenture facilitates financial access by providing simple mobile accounting and credit scoring tools for offline and unbanked individuals, the subject of this podcast.*

> *[From Media - Consult Hyperion]*[176]

Taken together, I think these provide compelling support to Kosta's intuition and it strikes a that, to use Jaron Lanier's term in "Who owns the future?", the "economic avatars" that arise at the intersection of the mobile phone and the social network may well prove to be more useful to a great majority of the world's population than their "official" identities, even if they have them, and indispensable to them if they do not. And, by the way, if you regard the whole idea of giving people credit on the basis of social capital as ridiculous and fanciful, I guess you didn't see this:

> *[Bogota] where Lenddo introduced a "social network" Visa card to 100,000 of its customers yesterday afternoon. By 4:00 p.m. today in New York, where the online lender for developing countries is based, more than 1,000 Colombians had applied for the card. Lenddo CEO and co-founder Jeff Stewart calls it the first time ever, anywhere, that approval for a credit card is based on applicants' reputations on Facebook, Google, LinkedIn, and Twitter.*

---

[176] http://www.chyp.com/media/podcast/shivani-siroya-inventure/

[From This Emerging Markets Credit Card Is Backed by Facebook Friends » Techonomy*]*

Identity is the new money, as they say. Well, as I say.

TAP into Nigeria (22nd July)

The Token Administration Platform, or TAP, is an e-voucher scheme that uses the latest tablet and smartcard technology to change the way the Nigerian government collects data and delivers benefits to its citizens. Its use of near field communication (NFC) technology is revolutionising agricultural development in rural Nigeria.

The International Fertilizer Development Center (IFDC) has signed up 470,000 farmers for GES Touch and Pay (TAP), an NFC-based service now live in the FCT and Sokoto states of Nigeria. The organisation hopes to have 500,000 farmers signed up in the coming weeks.

[From Nigerian farmers use NFC to access seed and fertilizer subsidies • NFC World+*]*[177]

The farmers are registered in support of the Nigerian Growth Enhancement Support (GES) scheme, where farmers and agricultural dealers have access to agricultural subsidies to drive production, output, and ultimately, the growth of the agriculture sector. Faced with inconsistent mobile coverage and the inefficiencies of paper-based systems, the Nigerian Government and a consortium of organisations, with funding from the UK's Department for International Development, are using TAP to transform the way agricultural subsidies in Nigeria are managed.

TAP is being used not only to register farmers for the GES, but also to accurately record and transfer biometric and credit data, and deliver vouchers to eligible farmers and agricultural dealers. TAP takes the discounts to the farmers by effectively extending mobile network coverage into an offline environment, beyond the current reach of mobile networks. And as is demanded of the most effective development initiatives, TAP vastly reduces the risk of fraud and ensures that fertiliser subsidies reach the farmers for whom they are intended.

Getting data back to the GES database using network coverage is slow, inefficient, and in some cases impossible. TAP's breakthrough architecture

---

[177] *http://www.nfcworld.com/2014/07/01/330078/nigerian-farmers-use-nfc-access-seed-fertilizer-subsidies/*

uses NFC and people-powered mesh networking to transfer data to field staff devices. Field staff can then send data to the GES database when they are back in network range and receive information to pass to offline agro-dealers about newly registered farmers.

Using a more secure, efficient and reliable process, TAP is directly supporting Nigerian farmers and boosting the local economy.

> *"TAP allows our farmers to redeem their inputs in areas where there are no networks, simply by using Android phones as smart cards...just tap it on the phone and all the allocation shows up and the farmers redeem their seeds and fertilizer without any network. It's revolutionary. We are the first in the world to do it."*
> *Akin Adesina, Minister of Agriculture for the Republic of Nigeria*

NFC is also used in farmer identification. Farmers are issued with a TAP contactless card, which is linked to the farmer's record via the tablet's NFC interface. The record includes a photograph of the farmer, which is subsequently presented to agro-dealers for verification at the time of voucher redemption.

> *"We are overcoming obstacles of geography, identity and fraud to quickly and effectively provide farmers in Nigeria the fertiliser subsidies they are entitled to and need, when they need them."*
> *Paul Makin (Head of Mobile Money Practice, Consult Hyperion)*

Although TAP is currently only active in Nigeria's Federal Capital Territory and Sokoto State, the initiative is already changing the agricultural landscape. In the first four months, TAP has now registered over 500,000 farmers; a near fivefold increase on the previous two years combined! In 2014, there will be more active users of contactless smartcards in Nigeria than the UK! The scheme will eventually involve more than 500,000 farmers and 100 agricultural dealers.

> *"TAP recognises duplicate registration and suspends farmers who have registered twice in an attempt to redeem double inputs. This is a huge benefit for agro-dealers like me."* *(Alhaji Idris Musa, Agro-Dealer)*

The TAP technology was developed by Consult Hyperion in partnership with international development specialists GRM International and the agricultural non-profit International Fertilizer Development Center (IFDC).

A few key points about the technology:

The Tomorrow's Transactions Reader 2015

Farmer registration details are captured electronically, including photos of the farmer and ID document thus reducing time, cost and errors.

Farmers are issued with a TAP card, configured using the NFC tablet.

Agro-dealers and registration officers transact electronically both in mobile coverage areas and offline.

Accurate data is returned to GES database within a week which allows faster settlement and loan repayments. This empowers private sector agro-dealers and gives lenders greater confidence in the scheme.

Automatic reports are generated detailing registrations and full transaction history (who, when, where, how much).

Fraud prevention and detection measures are integrated into the system and management processes.

Flexible back-office processes allow voucher schemes to be designed to meet the needs of the recipients, and not according to the limitations of technology.

TAP has been designed as a general-purpose, flexible, voucher registration, delivery and redemption platform. The team has already envisaged a range of potential applications for the platform, including: mHealth (where vouchers can be issued for vaccinations and other medication) and Education (where vouchers can be issued for training and other purposes, and redemption monitored in order to verify attendance). TAP's unique capability to link a sequence of vouchers across an extended time period can transform the way services are provided.

TAP allows development initiatives to be designed to meet the needs of the citizen, and not according to the limitations of technology. Follow #TAPnigeria and visit TAPnigeria on Flickr for more about this revolutionary innovation from the people whose lives are being changed.

Bill Gates was right at SIBOS, there is an identity problem (9th October)

SIBOS is SWIFT's annual conference and one of the fixed points in the banker's calendar. This year it was in Boston and one of its notable features was a closing keynote by Bill Gates, focusing on the issue of financial inclusion.

> *#Sibos Bill Gates @gatesfoundation tells bankers "developing #digital #Payments & identity systems key to help poor in developing countries"*

179

Brunella Lupano (@BLupano) <u>*October 2, 2014*</u>

Naturally, I couldn't help but notice the emphasis on digital identity as being equally as important as digital money in transforming the lives of the least well-off. The link between financial and social inclusion, as we at Consult Hyperion well understand because of our experiences going back many years, is strong. I commented on this three years ago, again (as it happens) in response to comment from Bill Gates.

> *People who are trapped in the cash economy are the ones who are most vulnerable to theft and extortion, most likely to lose their hard-earned notes and coins or have them destroyed by monetary policies, pay the highest transaction costs, lack credit ratings or references and (in an example I heard from Elizabeth Berthe of Grameen at the Forum this year) most likely to have their life savings eaten by rats.*

> *[From* <u>*Mobile payments are an important tool for financial inclusion - Tomorrow's Transactions*</u>*]*[178]

In the SIBOS speech, Bill Gates also said that the way that banks have traditionally made money cannot survive but that the necessary transition from analogue to digital financial services will address inefficiencies in the system, leading to (amongst other things) dramatically reduced transaction costs. He specifically pointed to the potential of blockchain technology to replace the banks' trusted role in the storage and transfer of value, which I thought was an interesting indicator of his thinking.

But back the point about identity.

When I ambled into SIBOS on the first day, I went to the registration desk and was asked to provide a photo ID. I had my wallet with me, so I took out my British driving licence (which they could not possibly verify, so it was a bit pointless) and gave it to the woman at the desk. Then I carried on tweeting or something. The woman at the desk handed me a badge and a bag and I went over to the entrance. They scanned my badge and waved me through and I went off to find the Innotribe room.

It was only after I sat down in the room that I noticed something odd about my badge. I had the badge for another David Birch! A David Birch from Hong Kong that I have never met although according to <u>LinkedIn</u> I do know some people who know both of us. Oh well, I thought. I'll go back to the desk and swap it for my badge. I wondered if the other David Birch had my badge or whether he had been arrested for trying to pretend to be

---

[178] *http://tomorrowstransactions.com/2011/04/mobile-payments-are-an-important-tool-for-financial-inclusion/*

me, or whatever. But then I thought - hell no, I won't go - as it will make for a **great blog post** about the importance of identity to be wandering around SWIFT's flagship event with the wrong badge on. Eventually, I thought, someone will pull me up and then I'll get the badge sorted.

They didn't.

So off I went to Innotribe in time for the discussion about Bitcoin. The discussion was a little narrow, as all the people on stage were Bitcoin believers, and I got into a bit of trouble on Twitter for making fun of some of their comments about Bitcoin replacing the dollar and such like.

I was accused of being "vile" on Twitter for saying this sort of thing, an accusation I refute in every degree.

[From Bitcoin, currency and competition at Tomorrow's Transactions.][179]

The next day, when I got to the conference and attempted ingress, the scanner flashed red and the gate staff told me I couldn't come in. So I went back to the registration desk and told them that my badge didn't work. So they gave me another one - exactly the same - and in I went.

On the third day I was supposed to be helping startups in the Innotribe area but I messed up my calendar and couldn't make it, so I asked our US Managing Director Howard Hall (who actually knows far more about the startup world than I do) to step in for me. I gave him the other David Birch's badge and off he went. The light went red and he was barred, so he did the same thing as me and went back to the registration desk where they gave him another copy of exactly the same badge - and in he went.

Next year I'll take along a British driving licence in the name of Satoshi Nakamoto and see how it goes.

Voting should be social, mobile, local (4th[th] December)

In many developed economies, and the UK is typical in this respect, there is great concern about the low turnout in national elections. Now, I am no expert on the topic, but I think it is reasonable to see that voters are becoming disenchanted with democracy. This may, I suppose, be a kind of societal sulk as democracy grows up (it is, after all, a relatively new way of organising human affairs for the great majority of people around the world). The electorate has gone up to its bedroom and started listening to music instead of studying.

---

[179] *http://tomorrowstransactions.com/2014/10/bitcoin-currency-and-competition/*

If politics is about giving voters what they want, you don't need experts and evidence, but just pollsters and market researchers.

[From Stumbling and Mumbling: Performativity in policy][180]

This is true, even if it is a counsel of despair. I'd prefer to get people to vote. Now, one line of thought (and I've touched on this before) is that society should make voting easier for people. The argument goes that if people can't be bothered to go round to a polling station (generally a local school in the English system) then perhaps we should find alternatives for them. After all, they vote in droves for drivel like "Britain's Strictly Got the X-Factor up the Jungle" and such like.

A new study published in Human Factors examines how smartphone-based voting systems can be incorporated into the current large-scale election process.

[From Smartphone-based voting technology may lead to fewer user errors | e! Science News][181]

I was very pleased to see this, because it is exactly what I wrote about before when I commented on the keynote talk I gave last year at the at the Fourth International Conference on e-Voting and Identity[182] (sponsored by Consult Hyperion and IBM UK), although my proposal wasn't quite the same because I don't think letting people vote at home is a good idea. How do you get around coercion and other kinds for fraud that would undermine democracy? So, I proposed letting people use some sort of voting app if they wanted to (perhaps the app could give them access to certain basic statistics such as the the amount we spend on interest on the national debt compared to the amount we spend on defence or the projected share of the national income that will be spent on pensions a decade from now, that sort of thing) but they still have to turn up in person (or be visited in person for people in, say, hospitals or care homes).

I show up with my phone and claim that I am entitled to vote: my phone presents a meaningless but unique number, this is entered manually or automatically into the polling clerk's phone which flashes up my picture if I am entitled to vote or a red cross if I am not.

---

[180]

http://stumblingandmumbling.typepad.com/stumbling_and_mumbling/2012/11/performativity-in-policy.html
[181]

http://esciencenews.com/articles/2014/02/26/smartphone.based.voting.technology.may.lead.fewer.user.errors
[182] http://www.voteid13.org/

182

[From Electronic voting, electronic identity, electronic entitlement][183]

This would not deal with the problem of people being too lazy to go and vote, but then I suppose if they are too lazy to go and vote then they get what's coming to them. If we reduce voting to people "liking" political parties on Facebook then we are in a dangerous place. Voting needs to take place in public. Having said that, we do need to make an effort to get young people into the habit of voting.

Electoral Commission calls for urgent reforms to engage younger voters who are turning out in declining numbers

[From UK should consider e-voting, elections watchdog urges | Politics | The Guardian][184]

Now, I certainly would not want to add any comment to this blog that might be construed as political, as that is not its purpose, but personally I'm not sure we want people voting when they are too young (under 21, say) because they don't know what they are talking about. In any case, I think it highly unlikely that a properly-architected electronic voting system would make much difference to whether young people vote or not.

Don't you wish voting were "more fun and social," in the parlance of social startups? Now, with a new collaboration between CNN and Facebook, it will be.

[From Facebook, CNN, and the Rise of Social Voting - Technology Review][185]

We live in a Venmo world now, so if the under-30s want to vote using an app that tells their friends that they voted, or perhaps even how they voted, or perhaps allows them to add a funny picture or an acute comment, well so be it. But make it secure, and make them go down to the polling station to use it.

---

[183] *http://tomorrowstransactions.com/2014/01/special-feature-electronic-voting-electronic-identity-and-electronic-entitlement/*
[184] *http://www.theguardian.com/politics/2014/mar/26/uk-e-voting-elections-electoral-commission-voters?commentpage=1*
[185] *http://www.technologyreview.com/view/428493/facebook-cnn-and-the-rise-of-social-voting/?ref=rss*

Glossary

2FA (Two Factor Authentication) – Authentication that uses two different mechanisms to verify identity for security purposes. An example of 2FA might require both a password and a smart card thus determining both what the user knows and what the user has.

API, Application Programme Interface. A set of specifications that software programmes can follow to communicate with each other

ATM, automated teller machine.

CNP, Card Not Present – A card payment via mail order, telephone or online where the retailer cannot see the physical card.

BLE, Bluetooth Low Energy.

CSP, Communication Services Provider.

DNS, Domain Name System – a hierarchical distributed naming system for computers, services or any resource on the internet or a private network.

ELMI (Electonic Money Institution Licence)

EMV (Europay, MasterCard and Visa) – A standard for Integrated Circuit Cards and their interaction with POS terminals.

eID (Electronic Identity Card)

GSM (Global System for Mobile communications) – The dominant international standard for digital mobile telephony.

HCE Host Card Emulation, a technique for enabling a computer or phone to emulate a smart card.

ISP (Internet Service Provider)

KYC (Know Your Customer) – Requirements in the form of due diligence and banking regulation applicable to companies dealing with financial transactions. The goal is for them to identify their customer correctly in order to help prevent identity theft fraud, money laundering and terrorist financing.

MiFare – Contactless smart card technology based on the ISO/IEC 14443 Type A standards developed by Phillips.

The Tomorrow's Transactions Reader 2015

MNO (Mobile Network Operator)

M-PESA – A mobile phone-based payment scheme in use in Kenya and now a number of other companies.

NFC (Near-Field Communication) – Wireless communication technology which allows data to be exchanged between two devices within a few centimetres each other.

NSTIC – National Strategy for Trusted Identities in Cyberspace.

Oyster – A contactless payment card used for train and bus tickets in the Greater London area of the UK.

P2P (Person-to-Person) – A financial transaction occurring directly between two people.

P2M (Person-to-Merchant)

PayPal – An online payment service.

PayPass (MasterCard) – The MasterCard brand for the contactless interface to their payment products.

PI (Payment Institution) – A new category of regulated financial institution created by the PSD

PIN (Personal Identification Number) – Usually a four digit number chosen by the user for authorization purposes when they try to access their account. The PIN is known only to the user and the system to allow a way for a machine to identify a valid account/card holder.

PKI (Public Key Infrastructure) -A set of hardware, software, people, policies and procedures needed to create, manage, distribute, use, store and revoke digital certificates.

POS (Point-of-sale or Point-of-service) – It can refer to a variety of definitions including the location of the retail establishment, or the specific counter, however it also could mean the hardware and software of the device used for the money transfer or (most often in this book) the terminal where the transaction occurred.

PSD (Payment Services Directive) – the legal foundation for the creation of an EU-wide single market for payments.

RFID (Radio Frequency Identification) – A family of technologies, which includes NFC, for zero-configuration data exchange between devices in proximity.

SCT (SEPA Credit Transfer) – The pan-European standard for "push" payments between bank accounts.

SE (Secure Element)

SEPA (Single European Payment Area) – A self-regulatory harmonisation project being introduced across the European payments market by banks with support from the European Commission (EC) and the European Central Bank (ECB). The SEPA initiative will encompass new, standard business and technical frameworks to make cross-border payments with the eurozone the same as domestic payments. The SEPA Credit Transfer went live in January 2008.

SIM (Subscriber Identity Module) – Is part of a removable integrated circuit card for mobile phones, the SIM cards securely store the keys necessary to identify the subscriber.

SMS (Short Message Service) – The mobile telecommunications network service used for text messaging.

UID (Unique Identity Number)

USIM (Universal Subscriber Identity Module) – A software application for UMTS mobile telephony, which runs on a UICC (an analog of a SIM card) which is inserted in a 3G mobile phone)

VRM (Vendor Relationship Management) - A category of business activity made possible by software tools that provide customers with both independence from vendors and better means for engaging with vendors.

Index

Google. *See*
Google Glass, 21
Government Banking
  Service. *See* GBS
Government Digital
  Service. *See* GDS
Grossman, Wendy, 53
hard ECU, 88
HCE, 151, *See*
Healey, Dennis, 25
Heinlein, Robert, 25
Hitachi, 11
Hochstein, Mark, 34
Host Card Emulation. *See*
  HCE
IBM, 182
ICB. *See*
ID card, 170
IDA, 31
Identification, 185
identity, 184
  crowdsourced, 176
  theft, 184
Identity Assurance
  Programme. *See* IDA
Identity is the New Money
  is the New Money, 30
identity management, 107
Independent Commission
  on Banking. *See* ICB
Innotribe, 181
Innovate Finance, 41
innovation, 129
Ireland, 27
Jacobs, Jane, 48
Kelly, Jordan, 39
King, Brett, 12
KYC, 36, 184
Le Bourget, 43

legal tender, 41
LinkedIn, 21
London, 48
  own currency, 50
loyalty points, 138
Lynch, Mike, 23
magnetic stripe, 109
Mann, Ronald, 13
MasterCard, 184, 185
MCX, 144
Merchant Customer
  Exchange. *See* MCX
Mobile, 184, 185
mobile phones, 186
mobile wallet, 135
M-PESA, 185
  Lipa Na M-PESA, 147
Nakamoto, Satoshi, 181
**National entitlement
  scheme**, 31, *See* NES
National identity scheme,
  31
National Payments Plan,
  31
Near-Field
  Communication. *See*
  NFC
NES, 172
New York, 47
NFC, 153
NSTIC, 185
Office of National
  Statistics. *See* ONS
online dating, 107
ONS, 25
Oyster, 185
Oyster Card, 19
P2P, 185
Passport, 20

Turkle, Sherry, 29
UnboundID, 20
Unconference. *See*
uranium, 59
US Postal Service, 47
VAT, 25
veins, 10
Venmo, 183
virtual account number.
  See VAN

Visa, 184
voting, 168
Weatherford, Jack, 30, 95
Western Union, 109
Will.i.am, 21
wine, 17
Winfrey, Oprah, 20
XS2A, 115